Perennials

THE BEST OF
FINE GARDENING®

Perennials

The Taunton Press

Cover photo: Roger Holmes

Back-cover photos: left, Roger Holmes;
top center, Lauren Springer; bottom center,
Roger Holmes; right, David Cavagnaro

Taunton
BOOKS & VIDEOS

for fellow enthusiasts

First printing: July 1993
Printed in the United States of America

A FINE GARDENING Book

FINE GARDENING® is a trademark of The Taunton Press, Inc.,
registered in the U.S. Patent and Trademark Office.

The Taunton Press
63 South Main Street
Box 5506
Newtown, CT 06470-5506

Library of Congress Cataloging-in-Publication Data

The Best of fine gardening. Perennials.
    p. cm.
    Articles originally published in Fine gardening magazine.
    "A Fine gardening book"— T.p. verso.
    Includes index.
    ISBN 1-56158-054-6
    1. Perennials. I. Fine gardening.
SB434.B46 1993   93-3150
635.9'32 — dc20   CIP

Contents

Introduction

Here are the best of all the perennials profiled by *Fine Gardening* magazine in its first five years of publication.

This collection includes hundreds of plants, clearly illustrated in photos and drawings. From ground covers to daylilies, veronicas to asters, perennials are great ornamental plants that return reliably every spring. Among them, you are sure to find many that are suited to your climate and growing conditions. They'll grace your garden and bring you years of pleasure.

You'll find the articles in this collection especially helpful and inspiring because they are the work of enthusiasts, gardeners who have grown the plants for years and want to help you enjoy them too. Sharing their hard-won experience, the authors tell you the climate and growing conditions each plant needs and explain how to use its shape, size, color and season of bloom to complement the design of your garden.

The editors of *Fine Gardening* hope you'll try the plants in this collection of articles. No matter which you choose to grow, your efforts will be rewarded.

"The Best of *Fine Gardening*" series collects articles from back issues of *Fine Gardening* magazine. A note on p. 96 gives the date of first publication for each article; product availability, suppliers' addresses and prices may have changed since then. This book is the first in the series. The next title is *Shrubs & Trees*.

The speckled, coppery orange flowers of 'Enchantment', a hybrid lily, crowd together in a rich display, while the slender buds promise more bloom to come. The stars of the summer garden, lilies are reliable perennials throughout much of the U.S.

A Lily Primer

Striking hybrids offer summer-long bloom

by Julius Wadekamper

I grew my first lily when I was six. My mother bought me three bulbs of the regal lily, which grows 6 ft. tall and bears 6-in. long, funnel-shaped flowers. One bulb never came up, and the second never bloomed, but the third had three glorious white flowers with a fragrance that filled the evening air. Lilies and their lovely flowers have played a big role in my life ever since.

Lilies are among the royalty of perennial plants. With their straight, green stems crowded with leaves and topped by profuse flower clusters, they have a commanding grace and beauty. Emerging each spring from a bulb deep underground, a lily adds new stems every year and soon becomes a striking colony. Lily flowers come in many forms and almost all colors except blue and purple, and by selecting different types, you can have bloom from early summer—as early as May—right through to fall. What's more, as cut flowers, lilies last up to three weeks, blooming until the last bud has opened. Best of all, gardeners from southern Canada to the mid-South—roughly USDA Hardiness Zones 3 (-40°F) through 7, and possibly farther south—can grow these beautiful flowers.

There are dozens of lily species and hundreds of hybrids. While many of the species are good garden plants (I recommend two on p. 12), the hybrids are generally easier to grow. I'll introduce you to four groups of hybrids—martagon, Asiatic, trumpet and Oriental. (For a list of mail-order lily nurseries, see Resources on p. 13.)

Lily (Lilium)

LIL-ee-um

- Tall, herbaceous perennials.
- Large, showy flowers atop erect, leafy stems.
- Flower colors include white, yellow, orange, pink, red; often spotted or striped.
- Full sun to partial shade, good air circulation.
- Well-drained, well-loosened, fertile soil.
- Regular moisture, but not constantly wet soil.
- Adapted in USDA Hardiness Zones 3 to 7 or southward, depending on type.
- Strongly vertical plants; suited to growing in borders; good cut flowers.

Four lily groups

Martagon lilies—The martagon hybrids are bred from species native primarily to the Caucasus, Germany and Czechoslovakia. Among hybrid lilies, as a group they are the earliest to bloom, flowering over a two-week period in early summer. Martagons have pendant flowers with backward-curling petals in colors ranging from white to yellows, oranges, pinks and deep wine-purple. Their leaves grow in whorls around the stem, not alternately scattered as on Asiatic and Oriental lilies. Martagons tend to be longer-lived than other lilies, and animal pests don't seem to bother them. They need mottled shade and slightly alkaline soil.

Asiatic lilies—By far the most popular hybrids, Asiatic lilies are bred from species native to China, Japan and Korea. Of all hybrids, Asiatics offer the greatest range of colors, the widest variety of flower types and sizes, and the longest season. In my Minnesota garden, a few cultivars flower even before martagons, but the height of the season is early July, and I still have bloom the third week of August. They're also good for cut flowers, as potted plants and for forcing. Some Asiatics face upward, others face outward, and still others are pendant. The pendant Asiatics resemble wild lilies and are well suited to cottage or old-fashioned gardens.

Trumpet lilies—The trumpets bloom in midsummer, a time when many perennial borders would otherwise lack color. Their deliciously fragrant flowers can be funnel-shaped, bowl-shaped, flat-faced or backward curling. One ancestor of this group is the species *Lilium henryi*. Its hybrid offspring are termed Aurelian lilies and have open, sunburst-shaped flowers, but they are considered part of the trumpet group. A clump of five or six trumpet lilies growing amid perennial grasses is spectacular. They are also beautiful among peonies, whose large, low leaves offer a green foundation for the towering lilies.

Oriental lilies—Perhaps the most exotic hybrids are the Orientals, derived from species native to Japan. Their flowers are large and open. Most Orientals have spotted flowers that are outward-facing or pendant, but some of the newest hybrids are upward-facing, and some are spotless, like the wildly popular 'Casablanca'. Orientals bloom over a long period—from mid-July into September in my garden. They have a pronounced sweet, spicy fragrance, which can be overpowering in a closed room.

Photo, facing page: Michael H. Dodge; illustrations: Rosalind Loeb Wanke

Growing good lilies

Planting time—The ideal time to plant lilies is fall, which is when nurseries dig the bulbs. Fall planting isn't always possible, however. Many Oriental and trumpet lilies mature quite late, and commercial growers cannot get them to market in time for fall planting in northern climates. These lilies should be purchased as soon as they're available in spring and planted immediately, since bulbs offered for sale in spring have been held in cold storage over winter.

Never buy lily bulbs that have been sitting for weeks in a plastic bag in the spring. Pale shoots curling around in the bag foretell sure death for the bulb. If you plant lilies in the spring, do so within two to three weeks of when they've been taken from cold storage, or before the shoots emerge.

Soil and fertilizer—Most lilies like their heads in the sun and their bulbs in cool ground. They need open, highly organic soil. Loosen the soil to 1 ft. and dig in lots of compost, leaf mold or peat. Aim for a soil that is 50% organic matter. Good drainage is a must—lilies won't tolerate soggy ground. If your soil is ill-drained, consider growing lilies in raised beds.

Asiatic and trumpet lilies tolerate a pH ranging from slightly acid to slightly alkaline. Of all lilies, Asiatics are the least fussy about soil texture, as long as drainage is adequate. I've grown them on soils from pure sand to heavy clay. Trumpet lilies also do well in almost any soil. However, their new shoots are very susceptible to late spring frost. It helps that they emerge later than other lilies, but if trumpets are up and frost is predicted, cover them. If they freeze, you'll be without flowers until the following year.

Martagon and Oriental lilies are more particular. Martagons prefer a pH of 6.5 to 7.6. In my garden, they do very well in a raised bed with limestone gravel as a ground cover. Oriental lilies, on the other hand, like acid soil, with a pH of about 5.5 to 6.5. You can lower the pH by adding peat, sulfur or ammonium sulfate. Orientals have a reputation for being difficult here in Minnesota, where our winter lows can be -40° F. I grow them successfully in a raised bed, in equal parts peat and soil. In winter, I mulch them with 8 in. of a straw-like grass. Here's a general rule of thumb about planting depth: measure the bulb's diameter and multiply by three; then

The pollen of 'Red Velvet' (above) turns brilliant yellow as it ages and contrasts strikingly with the deep burgundy-red flowers. Among Asiatic lilies, which are the easiest hybrids to grow, 'Connecticut King' (below) is one of the best.

Photos: above, David Cavagnaro; below, Michael H. Dodge

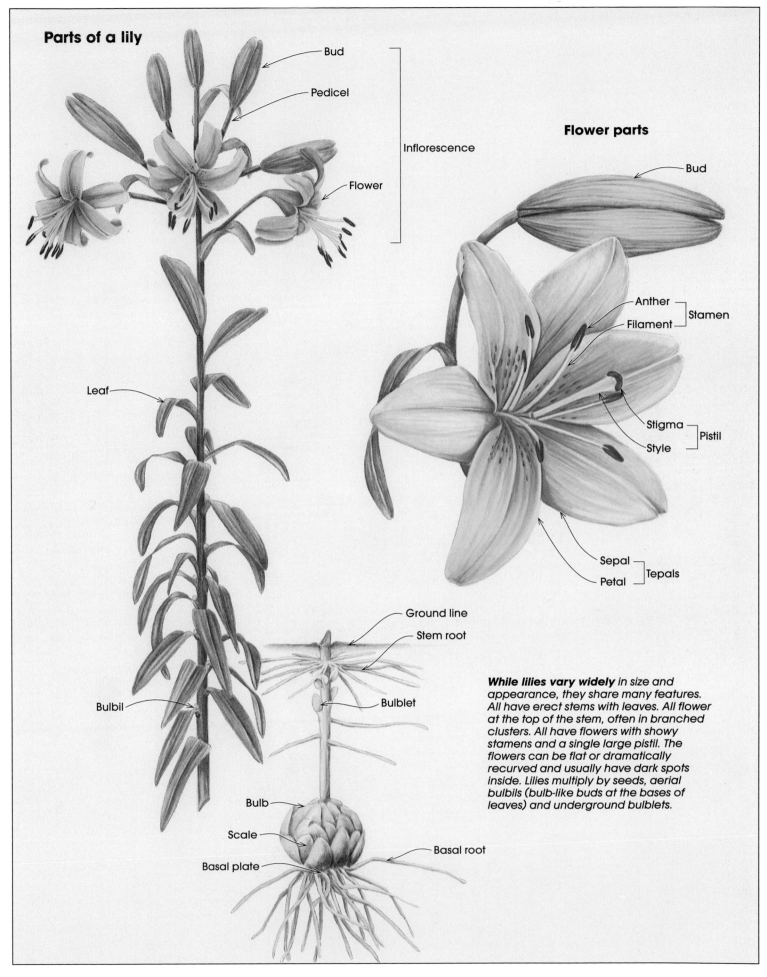

Parts of a lily

Bud

Pedicel

Inflorescence

Flower

Flower parts

Bud

Anther — Stamen
Filament

Stigma — Pistil
Style

Leaf

Sepal — Tepals
Petal

Ground line

Stem root

Bulblet

Bulbil

While lilies vary widely in size and appearance, they share many features. All have erect stems with leaves. All flower at the top of the stem, often in branched clusters. All have flowers with showy stamens and a single large pistil. The flowers can be flat or dramatically recurved and usually have dark spots inside. Lilies multiply by seeds, aerial bulbils (bulb-like buds at the bases of leaves) and underground bulblets.

Bulb

Scale

Basal root

Basal plate

A circle of white trumpets tops the stem of *Lilium regale*, one of the most easily grown species of lily. Highly fragrant, the flowers have yellow throats and purple-pink outer coloring. The stems stand up to 6 ft. tall.

Recommended lilies

There are hundreds of lilies on the market, but the author suggests you start with this list.

Martagon lilies

'Terrace City' strain—Light orange, pendant flowers, heavily speckled with brown; 4 ft. to 6 ft.; early summer. (While not genetically identical, members of a strain are usually quite similar.)

Asiatic lilies

'Connecticut King'—Upfacing, spotless, bright yellow flowers with a golden blush in the center; 3 ft.; early summer.

'Enchantment'—Nearly 50 years old and still popular; upfacing orange flowers, black spots. 3 ft.; early summer.

Trumpet lilies

'Moonlight'—Big, yellow flowers, greenish reverse; 4 ft. to 6 ft.; midsummer.

'Pink Perfection' strain—Outstanding strain, light to deep pink; 4½ ft. to 8 ft.; midsummer.

'White Henryi'—Award winner; sunburst-type white flowers, orange throats flecked with cinnamon; 4 ft. to 5 ft.; late summer.

Oriental lilies

'Black Beauty'—Virtually indestructible Oriental; deep red with green throat, strongly recurved; 5 ft. to 9 ft.; late summer.

'Casablanca'—Large, pure white flowers; 5 ft.; late summer.

'Imperial' strain—Orientals in shades of pink or red, white with lavender spots, and white with gold stripe; 6 ft. to 7 ft.; late summer.

Species lilies

Lilium henryi—Easy to grow. Dark-spotted, orange flowers; 3 ft. to 7 ft.; late summer.

L. regale—Another easy favorite. White trumpet flowers, lilac or purple outside; up to 6 ft.; midsummer.

plant to that depth. In heavy soils, plant slightly shallower; in light soils, slightly deeper. I space Asiatics 6 in. to 8 in. apart; trumpets 10 in. to 12 in. apart; and Orientals 12 in. to 15 in. apart. Martagons need even more room to multiply since you have to leave them in place—they don't take kindly to being dug up and divided.

Lilies are heavy feeders. I use a specially prepared 5-18-32 fertilizer, working in a small amount under the bulbs when I plant them. You can substitute a fertilizer with an analysis like 5-10-10 or 5-10-15, along with a little bonemeal or superphosphate, or use Osmocote, a slow-release fertilizer that is great for lilies. In the spring, spread the fertilizer on the soil around the plant, using about one tablespoonful per plant, slightly dug in. When the lilies are up and growing, I spray with Miracle-Gro, which contains trace elements; it gives my plants lush foliage and nice blooms.

Maintenance—Routine care includes controlling weeds and maintaining adequate moisture. Provide 1 in. to 2 in. of water a week if rain doesn't fall. I recommend a 5-in. to 6-in. organic mulch or a ground cover to suppress weeds and help keep soil moist—I like to plant petunias among my lilies. Deadhead regularly to keep seed pods from forming and to keep lilies vigorous.

In my experience, lilies rarely need staking. Even the trumpets, which can reach 8 ft. tall, usually have stalks stout enough to carry their flowers. If lilies are in partial shade, they may lean toward the sun. Stake them if you don't want them to tilt. Lilies growing in an unprotected, windy location may require support.

Many lilies benefit from being divided and moved to a fresh site from time to time. The Asiatics especially become overcrowded quickly; in my experience, they need to be moved every three or four years. Trumpets, on the other hand, are slow to feel crowded and don't start putting on their best show until they've been in place two or three years. Martagons don't like being moved at all.

No schedule can tell you the best time to divide lilies. Watch for signs of dwindling vigor, such as crowded stems and smaller plants and flowers. If your lilies are thriving, leave them alone. The preferred time to move Oriental and trumpet lilies is soon after the foliage dies down in fall. If you do it earlier, the bulbs will be puny and

Photos, these two pages: David Cavagnaro

under-nourished, but if you wait too long, they won't have time to develop new roots. Asiatic lilies can be transplanted in full bloom if you dig them with a ball of soil. I've done it hundreds of times, and the plants simply don't know they've been moved.

Problems—Lilies are tasty, succulent plants, and just about every four-footed pest likes to eat them. Rabbits chew the early shoots and leaves. Pocket gophers mine the bulbs. Deer browse on the flowers, and mice can also be a problem. In my garden, the Minnesota gopher—actually the 13-striped ground squirrel—is a serious pest; the young ones actually climb up the stems to chew the buds. The best solution to varmint problems is probably fencing in your lilies.

Well-grown lilies usually aren't bothered by disease; Asiatic and martagon hybrids are particularly disease-free. But under stressful conditions, problems can arise. One problem is basal rot, which occurs if drainage is poor. The basal plate of the bulb rots, and the scales fall away (for bulb anatomy, see the drawing on p. 11). Some cultivars are particularly prone to basal rot; those derived from *L. cernuum*, an ancestor of white and pink Asiatic lilies, are especially susceptible.

Botrytis leaf spot attacks aboveground lily parts. Leaves develop elliptical spots, and in severe cases flowers can be affected. There are essentially two ways to prevent botrytis—grow your lilies in an open area with plenty of ventilation so leaves dry off quickly after dew or rain, or spray regularly with a fungicide.

Lilies are susceptible to many viruses. Virus-infected plants show light streaks or mottling in the leaves, and foliage may be stunted or distorted. There's no cure—simply discard infected plants. To avoid the problem, buy virus-free bulbs from reputable growers and use good growing practices. If lilies appear weak, move them to a new location. Aphids can transmit viruses, so keep aphid populations on lilies and nearby plants under control.

None of these diseases has been a serious handicap for me in growing thousands of lilies. Basal rot and botrytis leaf spot are relatively easy to control with good growing practices. ☐

Julius Wadekamper grows and hybridizes lilies at his nursery, Borbeleta Gardens, located in Faribault, Minnesota.

The upright stems and orange flowers of an Asiatic hybrid lily tower above a shade garden. Lilies are strongly vertical plants that lend variety to many garden styles.

RESOURCES

If you're interested in lilies, consider joining the **North American Lily Society** *(NALS). A one-year membership fee of $12.50 brings quarterly bulletins, a 96-page yearbook, and access to slide and book libraries and round robins. Address: North American Lily Society, co Dr. Robert Gilman, P. O. Box 272, Owatonna, MN 55060. For further reading about lilies, you can order from the NALS* **Let's Grow Lilies** *by Virginia Howie, with line drawings, 1964, 52 pp.; $3.50 ppd. softcover.*

These mail-order nurseries specialize in lilies:

B & D Lilies, 330 P. St., Port Townsend, WA 98368, 206-385-1738. Catalog $3, deductible from first order.

Borbeleta Gardens, 15974 Canby Ave., Rte. 5, Faribault, MN 55021. Catalog $3.

Fairyland Begonia & Lily Garden, 1100 Griffith Rd., McKinleyville, CA 95521, 707-839-3034. Catalog 50 cents.

Hartle-Gilman, R R 4, Box 14, Owatonna, MN 55060, 507-451-3191. Price list free.

Honeywood Lilies, P. O. Box 63, Parkside, SK, Canada S0J 2A0. Catalog $1 deductible from first order.

This nursery, while not a lily specialist, offers hard-to-find martagon lilies:

Ambergate Gardens, 8015 Krey Ave., Waconia, MN 55387, 612-443-2248. Catalog $1.

Violets

Surprising variety from a familiar beauty

A carpet of Johnny-jump-ups blooms in rich profusion. Velvety texture and intense colors are found in many violet species.

by Ariel Haynes

I adore violets. They have a nostalgic air of innocence and the sweetness of unpretentious beauty. Their charm is redoubled by their great variety— among them they offer wonderful scents, an artist's palette of lovely colors, and beautiful foliage variations.

Violets are generally low-growing, shade-tolerant perennials. (I'm leaving out pansies, which are hybrid violets usually grown as annuals.) Most violets

Violets (*Viola*)

vi-OH-lah

- Low-growing perennial ground covers
- Most species prefer shade and moist soil; many are hardy to Zone 4
- Profuse flowers in many colors; some types intensely fragrant
- Generally herbaceous, but some evergreen species
- Spreading, sometimes invasive plants

are 4 in. to 8 in. tall, but some stand 14 in. tall, and others creep along, barely ½ in. off the ground. Many species are herbaceous and hardy to USDA Zone 4, while a few are evergreen in Zone 6 and southward.

Violet plants carpet the ground with color when they bloom. The flower colors are rich and varied—white, yellow, pale and deep blue, maroon, burgundy and deep purple, among others. All violets, from huge pansies to tiny alpines, have remarkably similar flowers, with a spurred lower petal and four upper petals in pairs which may differ from each other in size and color. Most species flower for

All photos: Balthazar Korab; illustration: Rosalind Loeb Wanke

several weeks in late spring, but some, such as the native bird-foot violet (*Viola pedata*), have smaller flushes of bloom through summer and into fall.

I am fascinated by the variation of form, texture and color in violet leaves. They can be heart-, spoon- or hand-shaped, rounded, toothed, fringed or dissected (cut into separate lobes, like the leaves of the bird-foot violet). Their size ranges from under ½ in. to 6 in. long, and their texture varies from delicate to substantial, with soft, fine hairs or satiny, even glossy, surfaces. Some violets have bold, crinkled or puckered leaves that are strongly reminiscent of hostas. Shades of fresh lime and pure green contrast with deep pine, blue-green and even purple, found in the Labrador violet (*V. labradorica*), which is prized more for the purple suffusion of its foliage than for its small, bluish flowers.

I use violets for ground covers, accents, and specimen plants. They are equally at home in open, deciduous woodland, meadows, shaded lawns or gardens, and shrub borders. I also grow a bed of fragrant sweet violets for cut flowers and winter salad greens (the leaves and flowers of violets are tasty, and the plants can be picked all year). My future plans include native violets in a flowering lawn, mountain dwellers in a rockery, and violet window boxes, to name just a few.

I started growing violets about seven years ago, when I dug a few clumps from my lawn and transplanted them to the garden. Since then I've collected nearly 50 species and cultivars, and my interest has become a passion. Almost anywhere in the U.S., you're likely to find several native species underfoot, growing in lawns, waste places or wild areas. You can dig your first clump for free, as I did, and if you catch the bug, you can collect new species and cultivars by mail (see Resources on p. 17).

Favorite violets

One of my favorite natives is the common blue violet (*V. sororia*), found throughout the eastern U.S. It is deciduous, with large, hairy leaves. The flowers vary widely in color—deep purple is common, but I have one that is near sky blue, and you can also find rosy tints, mauve, the occasional bicolor and white. The most familiar cultivar, 'Freckles', is white with a dusting of light purple speckles. (Some sources list 'Freckles' as a marsh blue violet, *V. cucullata.*) The woolly blue

At the feet of bearded irises in full bloom (above), Johnny-jump-ups (*Viola tricolor*) offer a counterpoint of texture and color. At right, the white, three-petaled flowers of trilliums rise above a solid ground cover of white-flowered Canada violets (*V. canadensis*).

violet spreads vigorously and can quickly move into a lawn, but I think that's one of its charms. I just mow as usual, and the plants stay short. If you want to control it, dig it up.

Another delightful native is the Labrador violet, which grows from Newfoundland to Alaska and is hardy to Zone 2. The deciduous plants are small—about 3 in. tall—and they occasionally rebloom. The flowers are generally bluish or lavender-purple and can vary from year to year. My plants were pale blue one season and rich lavender the next. (I moved the plant between seasons, but I don't know if that had any effect on the color.) The Labrador violet spreads with

and was a favorite of the Victorians for decorations and nosegays. The plants are hardy to Zone 7 and chancy in Zone 6. Violet lovers in the North often grow Parma violets in cool greenhouses and cold frames for winter bouquets, which can fill a house with fragrance. There are several cultivars and a range of flower colors.

Growing violets

Most violets prefer a moisture-retentive but well-drained soil. Some species, such as our native marsh blue violet, are quite tolerant of soggy soil conditions. In hotter, drier areas, most violets need a shady spot with only morning sun, and may need frequent watering.

Violets may also be grown in pots, using any good houseplant soil mixture that doesn't dry out too quickly. They must be kept cool—an enclosed

The stems of a hydrangea (above) emerge through a dense patch of 'King Henry', a violet cultivar with maroon flowers. Violets offer a range of colors, including the pure lemon of the downy yellow violet shown at right.

moderate vigor. It's wonderful grown as a lawn-like patch with spring bulbs coming up through it.

The bird-foot violet, a deciduous native of the Eastern U.S., likes well-drained conditions and full sun. The plants are 3 in. to 10 in. tall, with elegant, dissected leaves. There are two colors, white and purple, and two bicolors, purple over white and rich purple over mauve.

The sweet violet (V. odorata) is a European and Asian native long loved for the delicious scent of its foliage and flowers. Also called the English, garden or florist's violet, it is generally 4 in. to 8 in. tall, with 2-in. evergreen leaves. (I'm in the colder part of Zone 6, with unreliable snow cover, and my plants are evergreen without protection, although the leaves sometimes scorch.) Sweet violets exist in every shade of the violet spectrum, from the palest lilac pink through mauve, rose, crimson, and royal purple to true violet, periwinkle, pale sky blue and white. They bloom twice a year, roughly in spring and fall. Some have scattered flowers through summer, and a few will bloom right on through winter, especially if protected from crushing

snows and drying winds. Many fanciers grow them in unheated glasshouses or cold frames to have flowers in winter and non-stop bouquets. Unfortunately, the flowers of many modern cultivars lack fragrance, but you can still find fragrant types, and the leaves of all sweet violets are scented.

The double-flowered Parma violet is the most intensely scented of all violets. It's of uncertain hybrid parentage, but is related to the sweet violet. It was once grown on a large scale for perfume and cut flowers,

porch is ideal. Indoors, red spider mites can be a real nuisance, but frequent mistings keep them at bay.

Generally, violets flower best when they receive strong winter sunlight, but they will scorch in summer's midday sun, so the ideal location is under deciduous trees. Many will bloom well without direct sun, provided they get bright light.

To plant most native, sweet, and Parma violets, I add coarse sand and composted leaf mold, manure and peat to our acidic, clay soil. My sweet and Parma violets also get a dusting of lime to raise the soil pH. Set violets with the crown or rhizome at the soil line. They need to be firmly planted; tamp down well.

Outdoors, in most areas of the country, violets require little maintenance. The majority of species, if planted in a spot to their liking, need no attention. I have never bothered to feed or mulch my original "wild" violet beds, and they have grown thick and lush. However, violets bloom more bountifully if you fertilize, remove spent blossoms, and pinch runners in the spring. Extra care produces especially dramatic results from sweet violets, and even more so from Parmas.

Propagating violets

Violets are easy to propagate. The plants generally spread by rhizomes—underground stems—but a few species spread by runners—trailing stems that root and develop into new plants. You can start seeds, divide plants or transplant rooted runners.

To divide a clump of violets, dig up the roots 1 ft. deep and tease away a portion of the plant, including roots. If there is a rhizome, break off 1 in. or more (this is easiest in early spring). Violets with rhizomes are tough, and the pieces usually survive, even after the loss of their roots.

To propagate violets that make runners, first look for rooted offspring. Detach them, keeping a bit of soil around their roots. To encourage a runner to root, heap a bit of soil over the baby roots, firm it and wait a few weeks before digging up the runner for transplanting.

Starting violets from seeds is simple, but unpredictable. The seeds may germinate right away, or they may take 18 months. I usually let my plants self-sow. However, you can collect seeds, put them into the freezer for ten to 12 weeks, and sow them in a flat, which should be kept moist, cool and shaded.

Growing violets is one of my greatest joys. I love their subtle charm and quiet beauty, and I appreciate their versatility, hardiness and ease of care. They never make demands on my time and energy, and they don't suffer from neglect. The plants always bring me joy, especially when I see the face of a friend or family member light up at the gift of a potted violet or the first whiff of a sweetly scented bouquet. □

Ariel Haynes tends violets in Troy, Michigan.

Violets are spreading plants that love to creep across moist, shady lawns. Here, a colony of marsh blue violets holds its flowers above the grass.

RESOURCES

The author recommends these nurseries for plants of native and foreign violets.

Canyon Creek Nursery, 3527 Dry Creek Rd., Oroville, CA 95965. 916-533-2166. Catalog $1. *Sweet and Parma violets.*

Gardens of the Blue Ridge, P.O. Box 10, Pineola, NC 28662. 704-733-2417. Catalog $2. *Native violets.*

Lamb Nurseries, 101 E. Sharp Ave., Spokane, WA 99202. 509-328-7956. Catalog $1. *Sweet, Parma, foreign and native violets.*

Logee's Greenhouses, 141 North St., Danielson, CT 06239. 203-774-8038. Catalog $3. *Sweet, Parma and unusual foreign species violets.*

Russell Graham, 4030 Eagle Crest Rd. N.W., Salem, OR 97304. Catalog $2, refunded with order. *Sweet, foreign and native violets.*

For seeds of violet species and cultivars:

Chiltern Seeds, Bortree Stile, Ulverston, Cumbria, England LA12 7PB. Send check for $3 for catalog.

Thompson & Morgan, P.O. Box 1308, Jackson, NJ 08527. Catalog $2.

*Seeds of some species are offered by members of the **International Violet Association,** 8604 Main Rd., Berlin Heights, OH 44814-9620. Membership is $15 per year and includes a quarterly newsletter.*

A new book on violets is **Pansies, Violas and Violettas: The Complete Guide,** by Rodney Fuller, $36.95 ppd. from Trafalgar Square, P.O. Box 257, North Pomfret, VT 05053, 800-423-4525.

Perennial Asters
Stars of the flower garden

by Joseph L. Seals

Few hardy perennials yield such a lavish display of bloom as asters. Their beauty ranges from the quiet, unassuming charm of the small species to the almost overwhelming show of the tall, fall-flowering hybrids. Their diversity of flower color, size and habit lends them to use in nearly any garden, in nearly any site. And for me, an essential part of their beauty comes from their leniency: nothing could be easier to cultivate.

Asters are typical members of the daisy family (*Compositae*). What we call the flower is, in fact, a flower head composed of long, slender ray flowers (which look to our eyes like petals) radiating from a dense button of tiny, tubular disc flowers. The outer ray flowers can be white, pink, red, lavender or almost blue in color. The mass of central disc flowers is usually gold or orange. The overall effect reminded the Swedish botanist and taxonomist Linnaeus of a heavenly body, so he named this group of plants *Aster*—the Greek word for star.

The genus *Aster* is a large group of mostly perennial plants, the vast majority of which are winter hardy to USDA Hardiness Zone 4 (-30°F) [A few are hardy to Zone 3 (-40°F).] Botanists describe anywhere from 250 to 600 species of wild asters, most of them native to North American woodlands and fields. From a few of these wild species, plant breeders have developed hundreds of hybrids and cultivars.

Asters (*Aster* spp.)
ASS-tur

- Herbaceous perennials grown for their profusion of daisy flowers. The best known species and hybrids bloom in late summer or fall.

- Most are hardy to at least USDA Hardiness Zone 4 (-30°F). Many grow well in mild-winter climates.

- Flower colors range from white to pink to purple to almost blue.

- Height varies from the 8-in. tall rock garden species to the 4-ft. to 6-ft. tall fall-flowering hybrids.

- Grow in full sun in humus-rich, moist soil. Plants grown in hot-summer climates fare better in partial shade.

Asters have been in cultivation for centuries, but their rise to horticultural prominence dates only from the early 1900's. In 1907 an English nurseryman, Ernest Ballard, began breeding more compact, larger-flowered hybrids of the New York aster (*A. novi-belgii*), known in England as the Michaelmas daisy because it blooms at the time of the feast of St. Michael, the Archangel (September 29). They fell out of fashion after the Second World War, and are only now enjoying a renaissance of interest.

In addition to the familiar fall asters, I'll tell you about several of the more unusual species and hybrids. Over the last 20 years, I've grown many of them, first in California, then in the Midwest, with brief stints in the Pacific Northwest, Colorado, Texas and the Southeast. [For a much longer list of aster species, cultivars and sources, send $1 and an SASE to Kerry O'Neil, *Fine Gardening*, P.O. Box 5506, Newtown, CT 06470-5506.]

A constellation of asters
Gardeners think of asters as fall-flowering perennials, and fall is, indeed, the most common season of bloom, but there are asters that flower in the summer and even in the spring. If you grow a variety of species and cultivars, you can have asters blooming from late April through fall.

Spring and summer asters—My aster-flowering season starts with a refined little beauty from Europe called the rock aster (*A. alpinus*). Its violet-blue flowers open from late April to mid-May here in northern Illinois. The 2-in. wide flowers are large in proportion to the size of the plant, which, when in bloom, stands only about 8 in. high. There are several cultivars and a variety of flower colors. 'Goliath' seems to be the most commonly available. It grows taller than the species (to 15 in.) and bears soft blue flowers.

The rock aster can be finicky. Like

Illustration: Rosalind Loeb Wanke; photo, facing page: David Cavagnaro

Lavender New England asters cavort with nodding yellow goldenrods. Many asters are at their finest in fall, when other garden plants are growing weary.

The purple-red "petals" of the New York aster cultivar 'Crimson Brocade' surround a golden central disc. Like other daisies, aster flowers are actually flower heads composed of petal-like ray flowers radiating from a mass of tiny, tubular, yellow disc flowers.

Not all asters bloom in fall. Here, in spring, the violet flowers of *Aster tongolensis* explode into bloom next to a yellow madwort (*Alyssum*).

many alpine plants, it thrives in well drained, infertile soil in cool air. Where summers are warm or dry, planting in half-shade is a must.

In my garden, the second aster to bloom is *A. tongolensis*, a native of China. In May and June, it sends up stiff, 2-ft. tall stems, each bearing a solitary, pale violet-blue flower nearly 1½ in. in diameter. A good cultivar called 'Napsbury', which comes true from seed, has larger flowers than the species (up to 3 in. across); they're an intense purple-blue with vivid orange centers.

Another early flowering aster of note is *A. amellus*, the Italian aster or starwort (a name no longer used, but I like its charm). It grows to just under 2 ft. tall and bears single, large (nearly 3-in. wide), fragrant, lavender or pink flowers over much of the summer. The Italian aster has a reputation for being temperamental, but I've found that once it's established (which can take a few seasons), it's quite durable, drought-tolerant and long-blooming.

Summer-into-fall asters—Among garden asters, the types most commonly grown today descend from *A. dumosus*, a native of the eastern United States. The wild species ranges from 8 in. to 16 in. tall, has small, lilac-blue flowers and creeping rootstocks that are not overly aggressive. It isn't used much in gardens, but it's one parent (the other is often the New York aster) of a grand assortment of dwarf hybrids often listed in catalogs as New York asters. Worthy cultivars include 'Jenny', which bears double, violet-purple flowers on 16-in. stems in late August; 'Professor Kippenburg', popular for its wisteria-blue flowers on 15-in. stems in early September; and 'Royal Opal', which has ice-blue flowers with yellow centers on slightly shorter stems in September.

These asters make good ground covers, if you cut the plants back hard in the fall or early spring and apply a complete, but mild, fertilizer. In light soils, *A. dumosus* hybrids form a thick carpet that completely hides the soil surface; in bloom, the plants cover themselves with flowers. They are also useful on steeply sloping banks, both for ornament and for erosion control.

One of the most durable, yet delicate-looking, asters is the heath aster, *A. ericoides*. From late summer into fall, hundreds of small white flowers on wiry, 2-ft. to 3-ft. tall stems cover the plant. Light and graceful, heath

Photos: top, Chris Cheadle; below, Pamela Harper

The pink New England aster 'Alma Potschke' towers and tumbles over its dwarf white neighbor, *A. dumosus* 'Snowsprite'. Asters come in all sizes—from an 8-in. tall rock garden species to a 4-ft. to 5-ft. tall, fall-flowering hybrid such as 'Alma Potschke'.

asters make choice cut flowers. Several hybrids are available in a range of heights, flower colors and flowering times. Of these, 'Blue Star' is the easiest to find. It yields a cloud of 1-in. wide, pale blue flowers in late summer.

The heath aster is particularly easy to grow. And, unlike most asters, this species loves dry soil, perhaps because it is native to prairies and woodland edges. The only catch is that in warm areas the heath aster can become a serious weed because it sets seeds so prolifically.

Many gardeners believe that the finest of all asters is *A. × frikartii* (a hybrid between *A. amellus* and *A. thompsonii*, two European species). I'll come close to agreeing. Not only does this 2-ft. to 3-ft. tall plant bear fragrant flowers of the most exquisite lavender-blue, it also flowers profusely and for an exceptionally long time (July into October). But *A. × frikartii* has drawbacks. I've given up growing it because it has an ungraceful way of showing its distaste for my Zone 5 (-20°F) winters—it dies. You'll have

The exquisite lavender-blue flowers of *Aster × frikartii* 'Monch' nod above a low ground cover. Because 'Monch' flowers over an extraordinarily long period (July into October), many gardeners rate it as the finest of all aster cultivars.

better luck in mild-winter climes (I grew it to perfection when I lived in California). *A. × frikartii* is also particularly susceptible to root rot in wet soils.

The foremost cultivar of *A. × frikartii*, in my opinion, is 'Monch'. The clear, lavender-blue of its flowers is so gentle that it blends with almost any other color. The other widely available cultivar, 'Wonder of Staffa', has flowers that are a darker, less true, blue.

Fall asters—Asters traditionally have been used to fill out the garden in autumn—and no wonder. They intensify the fall garden better than any other group of plants, chrysanthemums aside. Too often, gardeners focus on spring color or are exhausted by the end of summer and unwilling to tend to a fall garden. So it's nice to have an end-of-season bonus from plants that don't require a great deal of care.

The splashiest asters of all come into their own in the fall. The best known is the New York aster, or Michaelmas daisy, and its numerous cultivars. Species plants grow from 2 ft. to 4 ft.

tall and in autumn bear clusters of violet-blue flowers. The variety of flower colors among the cultivars is almost infinite. My favorites include 'Crimson Brocade', which bears double, dark red flowers on 3-ft. stems; 'Marie Ballard', one of the oldest cultivars, still prized for its large, double, powder blue flowers on 4-ft. plants; and 'Patricia Ballard', which has double, carmine pink flowers on 4-ft. stems.

The other popular fall aster is the New England aster (*A. novae-angliae*). Because it flowers at about the same time as its New York relative, it, too, is often referred to as a Michaelmas daisy. But *A. novae-angliae* is a much taller plant, reaching a towering 6 ft. in height. Its flowers have more "petals" than those of the New York aster, which gives them a frillier look. The flowers also have a minor drawback—at night and on overcast days, they tend to close.

The New England aster has its share of cultivars. Here are three that offer blazing fall flower displays: 'Alma Potschke', with deep salmon-pink flowers on 4-ft. to 5-ft. plants; 'Harrington Pink', which bears pale pink flowers on 4-ft. stems; and 'September Ruby', which has deep rose-purple flowers and grows 3½-ft. tall. [For information about a new, low-growing cultivar of the New England aster called 'Purple Dome', see *FG* #25, p. 78.]

One introduced species, *A. tataricus*, seems right at home in the long, dry, sunny autumns of the Southeast. Although hardy to Zone 4, it thrives in heat and humidity and adapts readily to soil extremes from wet clay to dry sand (it may spread a little *too* rapidly in light soil, however). This species needs plenty of room; it grows 6 ft. to 8 ft. tall and just as broad. But its loose sprays of small, blue or violet-purple flower heads in luxuriant clusters make it worth the space.

Asters in the garden

Asters can play a variety of roles in the garden. I combine asters with all sorts of other plants, both perennials and annuals. The largest cultivars of both the New York and the New England asters serve as good backdrops for shorter plants. The smaller asters, such as the *A. dumosus* hybrids, are right at home as edging plants along the front of a perennial border. In a rock garden, the rock aster is an obvious choice, but many of the popular dwarf cultivars also make agreeable additions. They bring late-season color to gardens that usually are most showy in spring. All mounding asters look great in the company of ornamental grasses such as *Panicum*, *Pennisetum* and *Miscanthus*; the spreading, cushion form of the asters contrasts nicely with the arching stems of the grasses.

I particularly like combinations of blue and pink. The blue cultivars of the New York and the New England asters and *A.* × *frikartii* provide the perfect complement to almost anything pink. My favorite aster mates include Japanese anemones (I like the cultivar 'Margarete'), *Lavatera olbia* 'Rosea' and fall-flowering sedums, such as *Sedum* 'Autumn Joy' and pink *S. spectabile* cultivars.

No meadow seems complete without asters. The species asters can naturalize and grow and topple without restraint while adding a striking splash of color to what might otherwise be an uninteresting view. Even the urbane cultivars appear right at home in peripheral areas, in waste places or where the garden meets the wilds.

Growing asters

Asters prefer a deep, reasonably light, moderately fertile soil. During the active growing season, don't allow the soil to become overly dry (which, odd as it may sound, encourages the growth of powdery mildew), and during the dormant season, keep the soil from becoming soggy to prevent the roots from rotting. Most asters prefer full sun, but many cultivars seem to show their best flower color in partly shady sites, especially in the South.

Asters are sometimes plagued by fungal diseases. The most common are wilt disease, which causes the leaves of entire stems to yellow and wilt; powdery mildew, a white, felty film that covers leaves and stems; and botrytis, a gray fuzz that appears mostly on buds and flowers. All three of these diseases are aggravated by excessive nutrient levels in the soil. You can reduce the incidence of disease by planting asters in soil rich in organic matter (organic matter tends to release its nutrients slowly), by mulching them and by fertilizing them only sparingly, if at all. Growing asters in open garden areas where the air circulates freely also helps prevent disease problems.

Tall asters may require staking to stop them from toppling over in a stiff breeze or a downpour. If you want more compact, free-blooming plants, pinch the growing tips back once or twice before mid-season. I usually make a first pinch when the plants are 6 in. tall, and then I pinch again about a month later—but no later than July 4.

Aster species and some of the cultivars produce a bounty of seedlings. If you don't want the volunteers clogging your garden, you'll have to deadhead—remove faded flowers regularly before the seeds have a chance to mature and drop.

Because plant clumps left to themselves tend to spread and die out in the center, most asters require frequent division. I recommend you divide vigorous asters at least every three years—every year if you want to keep them at their most magnificent. The best time to divide asters is in the spring, but you can divide the spring- and early summer-flowering species in late autumn after they've flowered. Replant only rooted, vigorous pieces—three to five shoots to each piece—from the outside of each clump, where growth is most active. □

Joseph L. Seals is marketing manager of Ball Seed Company. He gardens in Wheaton, Illinois.

SOURCES

The first place to look for asters is your local nursery, where you're likely to find a selection of asters that grow well in your area. The following mail-order nurseries carry many of the asters described by the author.

Bluestone Perennials, 7211 Middle Ridge Road, Madison, OH 44057, 800-852-5243. Catalog free.

Busse Gardens, Rte. 2, Box 238, Cokato, MN 55321-9426, 612-286-2654. Catalog $2, deductible from first order.

Carroll Gardens, 444 East Main Street, P.O. Box 310, Westminster, MD 21158, 301-848-5422. Catalog $2, deductible from first order.

Lamb Nurseries, 101 E. Sharp Ave., Spokane, WA 99202, 509-328-7956. Catalog $1.

Milaeger's Gardens, 4838 Douglas Avenue, Racine, WI 53402-2498, 800-669-9956. Catalog $1.

Andre Viette Farm & Nursery, Rte. 1, Box 16, Fisherville, VA 22939, 703-943-2315. Catalog $3.

Growing Hardy Cyclamen

Delicate color throughout the year

by Sharon A. Shreet

Summer wanes, the bees have long since abandoned the lavender, and the fragrance of lilies lingers only in my memory. It's time to turn my attention to the winsome, blushing blossoms of hardy cyclamen soon to appear at the edges of my woodland garden. Their fragrant pink and white flowers help me fend off the bleakness of impending winter.

Hardy cyclamen are not widely grown in the United States. I think many gardeners imagine the hardy cyclamen to have the same needs as the fussy florist's cyclamen, but in fact, the hardy types are of easy culture. Five of the 19 species are hardy to Zones 4 or 5, and several others are hardy to Zones 6 or 7. If you haven't already tried them, you should treat yourself to some hardy cyclamen.

Cyclamen are native to parts of Europe and western Asia, as well as North Africa. These plants have been cultivated for their ornamental and herbal uses since the 1500s. Eating powdered cyclamen leaves was once believed to make a man amorous, and the mere sight of a cyclamen blossom by a pregnant woman was reputed to hasten her baby's birth.

Hardy cyclamen grow from tubers, which can live as long as 60 years. There are documented cases of *C. hederifolium* living over 100 years and reaching diameters the size of dinner plates. Plants of that size may bear 50 flowers at a time. The plants reach 3 in. to 6 in. tall and look like diminutive versions of the florist's cyclamen. Hardy cyclamen species each bloom for several weeks, and at various times of the year. With careful selection, you can have an almost-continuous

Although delicate looking, hardy cyclamen push through layers of autumn leaves, and sometimes snow, to bloom during the cold months of the year. Here, the magenta-flowered *Cyclamen coum* and the white-flowered *C. coum* 'Album' blossom together.

show of cyclamen throughout the year. The plants send up flowers that twist and arch their petals backward in shades of carmine, dark to light pink, white flushed with pink, or pure white. The blossoms appear delicate, yet they withstand cold weather and remain intact even after downpours in my Maryland garden (USDA Zone 7). During the winter of 1990, my plants went right on blooming despite a cold spell with temperatures in the teens.

The heart-shaped leaves of most hardy cyclamen are splashed with a delicate, white tracery, and range from 1 in. to 5 in. across. Most species send up leaves first, then flowers, but one, *C. hederifolium*, blooms before its leaves appear. As the blossoms fade, the flower stems of most species coil tightly to carry their seed capsules to soil level. After the seed capsules reach the ground, the leaves spread over them, sheltering the ripening seeds

Photos: Pamela Harper

After the plant has bloomed, cyclamen leaves form an attractive groundcover until summer's heat forces the plant into dormancy. Here *Cyclamen hederifolium* grows alongside 'Red Wing' azaleas and an evergreen groundcover called inside-out flower.

and creating a dense mat of foliage. This attractive groundcover lasts until summer's heat forces the plant into dormancy.

Reliably hardy cyclamen

Five species are reliably hardy in most of the United States (see chart at right). *C. hederifolium* (once called *C. neapolitanum*) blooms in my garden from mid-October through Thanksgiving. But, in most of the country, *C. hederifolium* blooms occasionally in summer, peaking as early as late August. Its elegant, elongated 1-in. flowers are rose-pink or white. *C. hederifolium* is followed in early February (or, in some years, as early as late December in my garden) by *C. coum*, which sometimes blooms from beneath a cloak of snow. There are several forms of *C. coum*, blooming in carmine, pink or white. All have somewhat shorter, stockier flowers than *C. hederifolium*, and many have magnificently variegated leaves marked with silver or cream. *C. purpurascens* is a nearly-evergreen plant, loosing some of its leaves just as new ones emerge in March. It carries its pink or magenta flowers from late summer into autumn in my garden. In other areas, *C. purpurascens* may start flowering by late May. Its blossoms are shaped like the blossoms of *C. hederifolium*, and have a delightful fragrance.

C. intaminatum blooms October through December. This species is smaller than other cyclamen plants, and has pink or white flowers and rounded, beautifully variegated leaves. *C. cilicium*, another hardy species, has deep pink to white flowers in late fall and variegated leaves.

Hardy Cyclamen
(*Cyclamen* spp.)

- Tuberous perennial
- 3 in. to 6 in.tall
- Blooms at various times of year in shades of carmine, pink, and white
- Shade to part shade
- Well-drained, humus-rich soil, moderate pH
- Use in perennial, woodland and shaded rock gardens
- Hardy in Zones 4 or 5 through 9, depending on species

Semi-hardy cyclamen

Although I grow mostly the hardy species, I have tried several cyclamen that are semi-hardy and which should grow well in USDA Zones 6 or 7 through Zone 9. *C. pseudibericum* has done well for me. This spring-blooming cyclamen has heart-shaped, toothed leaves and pink flowers; both its leaves and flowers are larger than those of *C. coum*. *C. balearicum*, a spring bloomer, is one of the smallest-flowered species in the genus. Its fragrant, white or off-white blossoms have pink veins. Its leaves are grayish green, blunt-ended and sometimes have rolled edges. I've started *C. balearicum* from seed, but it hasn't wintered over yet, so its hardiness is untested in my garden. *C. mirabile* blooms October through December. It has somewhat angular leaves, sometimes with pink markings, and fringed, pink flowers.

Cyclamen in the garden

Used in quantity, hardy cyclamen capture attention even from a distance. But they are best planted where the unique character of their small flowers and low-growing foliage can be enjoyed at close range. I suggest planting hardy cyclamen near an often-traveled walk or steps. If you don't mind venturing out in winter, try planting hardy cyclamen in a rock garden or along a wooded path. I especially like them planted in front of low, small-needled evergreen shrubs, such as bird's-nest spruce, blue star ju-

Hardy and semi-hardy cyclamen species

Those shown as "hardy" will grow in Zones 4 or 5 through 9; those shown as "semi-hardy" can be successfully grown in Zones 6 or 7 through 9. All grow best in partial shade unless otherwise noted.

Species	Hardiness	Characteristics
C. cilicium	Hardy	Deep pink to white flowers in late autumn; variegated leaves; needs some sun.
C. coum	Hardy	Many forms; flowers in winter in all shades; solid or variegated leaves.
C. hederifolium	Hardy	Pink or white flowers in autumn; leaves green or variegated; very easy to grow.
C. intaminatum	Hardy	Miniature plant; pink or white flowers in late autumn; leaves green or variegated; tolerates sun.
C. mirabile	Semi-hardy	Fringed pink flowers in late autumn; beautifully variegated leaves; tolerates sun.
C. purpurascens	Hardy	Fragrant rose-pink flowers in summer; leaves green or variegated; plant is never dormant; shade.
C. pseudibericum	Semi-hardy	Pink flowers in spring; heart-shaped, toothed leaves; tolerates shade.
C. balearicum	Semi-hardy	Small, fragrant, white or off-white blossoms with pink veins in spring; grayish-green leaves; shade.

Illustration: Rosalind L. Wanke

niper, or dwarf cedar. The evergreens provide a nice backdrop for the cyclamen blossoms, as well as color and texture contrast for the foliage.

Hardy cyclamen require humus-rich soil and, above all, good drainage. Drainage is never a problem in my sandy soil, but I always work in several shovelsful of compost or peat moss before planting. Adding gravel to clay soils will improve drainage. In their native lands, hardy cyclamen are often found growing in alkaline soils, but these plants aren't fussy about soil pH. They grow well in my slightly acidic soil among native hollies and dogwoods. In general, cyclamen thrive in areas that receive morning sun or day-long, dappled sunlight. Exceptions include *C. balearicum* and *purpurascens*, which need shade, and *C. coum*, which needs summer shade (see chart on opposite page).

Hardy cyclamen may be set out either as growing plants or as dormant tubers. Set out plants in spring or fall; dormant tubers should be planted in July or August. Plants are generally more expensive than tubers, but you may find the extra expense worthwhile. The tubers have an annoying habit of remaining dormant for so long that you may suspect they were dead when you planted them. After I planted my first cyclamen tubers, I saw no evidence of them for two years. Unaware of their tendency to remain dormant for so long, and knowing that hardy cyclamen were once commonly called "sowbread" because of their use as pig food, I thought that perhaps the neighborhood squirrels had found a similar use for mine. I regained some hope after reading Allen Lacy's account of waiting for hardy cyclamen to bloom (which had a happy ending) in his book, *Home Ground*. Just a few weeks later, I was delighted by the sight of my first cyclamen blossoms.

When you plant, handle cyclamen carefully to avoid breaking the roots. Set plants at the same level they were growing in the nursery. Except for a couple of species, the tubers should be planted with their tops about 2 in. below the soil surface. Plant tubers of *C. hederifolium* at soil level; *C. cilicium* should have the surface of its tuber just above soil level. Before planting dormant tubers, you must first find the top. That is the hardest part of growing hardy cyclamen (and another reason to choose started plants over tubers), because the top of a

tuber is not easily distinguishable. The tubers frequently have a flat or slightly depressed top and a more rounded bottom. A tuber of *C. hederifolium* has roots mostly on its top half; *C. coum*, mostly on its lower surface; and *C. purpurascens*, all over. In the end, you may just have to wish yourself luck, hold your breath and guess.

Whether you choose plants or tubers, chances are that they won't

Cyclamen cilicium has slender pink or white flowers, which occasionally have strikingly-twisted petals. Its leaves are small and spoon-shaped.

SOURCES

The Cyclamen Society offers rare and unusual seed to its members. For information, write: **The Cyclamen Society**, *c/o Dr. David Bent, 9 Tudor Dr., Otford, Sevenoaks, Kent TN14 5QP, England.*

The author suggests the following sources for hardy cyclamen seeds, tubers and plants.

Montrose Nursery, P.O. Box 957, Hillsborough, NC 27278. 919-732-7787. Cyclamen specialists, offering seeds and nursery-grown plants of many species and forms. Catalog $2.00.

McClure and Zimmerman, 108 W. Winnebago, P.O. Box 368, Friesland, WI 53935. 414-326-4220. Nursery-grown dormant tubers. Catalog free.

Thompson & Morgan, Inc., P.O. Box 1308, Jackson, NJ 08527. 201-363-2225. Offers seeds. Catalog free.

bloom much their first season. Hardy cyclamen resent transplanting. Once established, however, they are free-blooming and undemanding. They require no attention during the summer, though I've found that a topdressing of compost each June is beneficial. From September through May, when the plants are actively growing, I give them an occasional soaking because my soil is sandy and well-drained. This is not advised for heavier soils, however. Frequent rains in my area generally provide all the water needed. I water them only if we have had no rain for two or three weeks and the ground remains unfrozen.

Starting from seed

Seed is cyclamen's only means of propagation. And fortunately for gardeners like me who want more plants than they could afford to buy, hardy cyclamen are moderately easy to grow from seed. Happily-situated cyclamen sometimes increase their colonies by self-seeding. More often, though, ants carry away the sticky seeds. So I intervene, collecting the seeds when they ripen in late spring. I store them in a cool, dry place until I'm ready to plant them in flats in July or August. Hardy cyclamen seeds also may be purchased by mail (see Sources at left).

Cyclamen seeds are like little nuggets, smaller than peppercorns, but just as hard. I soak them in water for 24 hours before planting to soften the seed coat. Then I sow the seeds about 1 in. apart on a moist mixture of two parts potting soil, one part peat moss, and one part sand. Next I sprinkle over a thin layer of sand and cover the trays with Reemay (a stiff, gauze-like fabric available from Gardener's Supply Company, 128 Intervale Road, Burlington, VT 05401). I sink the trays to their rims in a shady part of my garden.

Keep the seeds constantly moist, but not soaking wet, until they germinate, which can take a year or more. The seeds usually germinate the following spring or fall. Covering trays with plastic, then newspaper, and keeping them in a cool basement increases germination. When the plants have developed tiny tubers, I place them in individual pots or in a seedling bed. They begin to bloom about two years after planting out. □

Sharon A. Shreet gardens and grows hardy cyclamen in Arnold, Maryland.

Herbaceous Peonies

Cold-hardy perennials with spectacular blooms

by David Harrap

The peony is the only cultivated herbaceous perennial I've grown that can withstand the severe cold of the Canadian prairie provinces, yet still produce magnificent blooms year after year. I can say this with confidence after 14 years of gardening in Edmonton, Canada, where winter temperatures often plunge to -40°. (It's cold at this temperature, no matter if it's measured in centigrade or Fahrenheit!) I've even heard reports of peonies thriving farther north than here, in Fort Simpson, about 700 miles north of Edmonton. (U.S.D.A. Hardiness Zone 1). They also can be grown south of here, through Zone 7 and sometimes into Zone 8. Farther south, winters aren't cold enough to induce dormancy, and summers are so hot that plants usually don't do well for very long. (See box on p. 28 for more on growing peonies in the South.)

Grown under proper conditions, peonies have been known to bloom year after year for half a century or more, filling the garden with flowers ranging in color from vibrant reds to delicate pastels to pure white. Many cultivars are fragrant, as well. Add to these virtues rich green, glossy leaves, a neat growth habit and long life as cut flowers, and it's no wonder that peonies have been regarded as the king of flowers since ancient times.

My earliest memories of peonies are from the garden of my childhood, nestled among lime-green beeches and the gently rolling Chiltern Hills of southern England. There were formal rose beds, fruit and vegetable gardens and perennial borders, but I remember the peonies most of all.

I particularly remember a large crystal bowl of peony flowers that sat on a Victorian table in the lounge. Sun streaming through leaded windows lit up the flowers as if they

Peony (*Paeonia* spp. and hybrids)

- Herbaceous perennial with fleshy roots
- 14 in. to 3 ft. tall, depending on cultivar
- Spring flowers in shades of red, pink, cream and white
- Full or part-sun
- Well-drained soil, good air circulation
- Regular moisture
- Hardy in USDA Zones 2-7 or 8
- Use in perennial borders

were on fire. Day after day, the all-pervading fragrance from 'Sarah Bernhardt', 'Duchesse de Nemours', 'Kelway's Glorious', 'Edulis Superba' and 'Lady Alexandra Duff' filled the house.

How my father doted on the peonies, giving them the very best of his attention. After his death, the untended garden became overgrown with weeds, but the peonies faithfully bloomed every year, looking nearly as good as ever. Thirty-four years later, my love for these flowers has not diminished. I even grow some of those old varieties that filled my mother's bowl. For when you fall in love with a flower, it's for a lifetime.

Meet herbaceous peonies

If you find established peonies in your garden, they're likely to be herbaceous, rather than the less common, but equally attractive, shrub-like tree peony.

Peonies' neat growth habit and luxuriant flowers recommend them for large and small landscapes alike. Pictured from front to back above are red-flowered 'Barrington Belle', white 'Baroness Schroeder' and pink 'West Elkton'; and, on the facing page, 'Doreen'.

Photos, except where noted: Allen Rokach; illustration: Rosalind L. Wanke

(See *Fine Gardening* #14, July/August 1990, pp. 22-26 for more on tree peonies.) Early each spring, herbaceous peonies send up many dark red stems from a fleshy rootstock. Plants reach about 14 in. to 3 ft. tall during the growing season, depending on the cultivar. They form slowly-expanding clumps. Many peonies have dark green, lustrous, smooth leaves, but leaf color may range from mint-green to deep olive. Peony foliage retains a handsome appearance throughout the growing season, sometimes taking on a beautiful maroon color toward the end of summer.

Peonies really command attention when they bloom. Their flowers, which can reach 5 in. in diameter, range from simple, single types, with a layer of distinct petals encircling a cluster of stamens, to more complex doubles, whose billowy mass of petals completely hides the reproductive parts. Japanese and semi-double flowers are intermediate in form. Those sold as anemone types are either doubles or Japanese.

Flowers are borne singly near the top of the stems and also grow from side buds. Cultivars are classified as early, midseason- or late-blooming. In my garden, the bloom period is from about the end of May through June; farther south the early-bloomers open in late April. All the flowers on an individual plant open at nearly the same time, and plants stay in bloom for two to three weeks, as long as they aren't battered about by heavy wind or rain.

Hundreds of cultivars and several herbaceous peony species are commercially available. A tremendous amount of hybridization over the past 50 years has produced cultivars with stronger stems and larger flowers in more vibrant colors, including shades of red, pink, salmon, coral, yellow, cream and white.

Peony flowers encompass a diversity of forms and colors, ranging from (above) 'Soft Salmon Saucer' and, on the facing page, 'Ivory White Saucer' (top right), a crimson cultivar (top left), and 'Bev' (bottom).

The Chinese peony (*Paeonia lactiflora*), a white, single-flowered peony native to Tibet, Manchuria and eastern Siberia, is parent to most of our garden cultivars, including beautiful old aristocrats such as 'Monsieur Jules Elie', 'Festiva Maxima', 'Edulis Superba', 'Reine Hortense' and 'Sarah Bernhardt'. All have double flowers in shades of white or pink; some are fragrant.

P. officinalis, a southern European native with single, scarlet flowers, is rarely available as a species, but many of its double-flowered cultivars, such as the white 'Alba Plena' and red 'Rubra Plena' are readily available.

The fernleaf peony (*P. tenuifolia*) and its cultivars are becoming more popular. Because they have poppy-like flowers and fennel-like leaves, one could be forgiven for thinking they are anything but peonies. Once I grew 'Flora Plena', a dark red, very early-flowering cultivar that survives our harshest winters, but have decided this peony is not for my garden—its blooms were fleeting and the foliage deteriorated by mid-summer, a characteristic of some, but not all, fernleaf peonies.

In the garden

With such a wealth of attractive foliage, peonies are appealing even when planted as single specimens. However, in a postage-stamp garden such as mine—my entire lot is a mere 118 ft. long by 25 ft. wide, including a 1000-sq.-ft. house—plants are never far from their neighbors. Fortunately, their tidy foliage and non-invasive habit makes peonies well-suited for a small site. I've dotted more than 35 peonies around the front and back flower borders, tucking small groups of them among other perennials such as hostas, delphiniums, bergenias, lilies, hardy shrub roses, daylilies, bleeding-hearts and phlox.

Peonies lend themselves to many attractive combinations. In my garden, the silvery-white, deeply-cut leaves of dusty miller provide a pleasing contrast to the deep green peony foliage. Elsewhere, tall delphiniums and lilies form an ideal backdrop for the lower-growing peonies. With a little encouragement, the lily stems serve double-duty as a support for the flower-laden peonies. Blooming among the vivid orange flowers of the Asiatic lily 'Moulin Rouge', the soft pastel colors of several old Chinese peonies seem to quiet its fiery color. Peony foliage also provides the perfect cover-up for the dying foliage of spring-flowering bulbs.

Growing peonies

Site selection—Peonies need a sunny, well-drained site free of competing roots, and good air circulation. I avoid plant-

---

Growing herbaceous peonies in warm climates

by Nancy Beaubaire

The best climate for growing peonies provides them with enough winter cold to induce dormancy and not too much heat and humidity at flowering time. If apples do well in your microclimate, it's probably cold enough for peonies. Most experts don't recommend growing peonies in climates with winters warmer than USDA Hardiness Zone 7 or 8, (winter lows of 0° to 20°F). Use this as a guide, but remember that a northerly Zone 8, such as Oregon, may be favorable for peonies, while a southerly Zone 8, such as South Carolina, may not. The American Peony Society doesn't recommend growing them south of Birmingham, Alabama. In the deep South, where two or three months of hot, humid weather are common, peonies frequently fail to bloom, and often the plants don't survive beyond a few years—hardly a

worthwhile investment for a plant that has great potential for beauty and longevity when grown under the proper conditions.

But if you garden in a borderline climate and want to try peonies, here are a few hints from some nurseries that specialize in peonies. Buy early-blooming hybrids that flower before the onset of hot weather, and select those with single or semi-double flowers. Plant peonies in a cool site in part-shade. Enrich the soil generously with organic matter and mulch the plants deeply. Set the divisions with the eyes at ground level so they catch the slightest nip of frost. Check with nurseries that specialize in peonies, your state university Cooperative Extension Service and your neighbors for the best cultivars and techniques for your area.

Nancy Beaubaire is an associate editor at Fine Gardening.

ing peonies within a few feet of the house, where the warmer soil encourages tender new growth before the danger of late spring frosts has passed. My east-facing border has proved to be one of the best exposures—the soil warms up early in the spring and the plants bloom before the onset of summer heat. Those planted in a west-facing location bloom later, enabling me to slightly extend the blooming season of the same cultivar by planting it in two different exposures.

Buying peonies—Peonies are best planted when they are dormant and before

the ground freezes. (See Resources below for a list of mail-order nurseries.) They are slow-rooting plants. If planted in warm, spring weather, shoots grow before the roots become established, and the plants soon wither and die. I plant in September and October; gardeners in milder climates can plant through November. Pot-grown peonies can be set in the ground at any time, providing they have an abundance of fine roots to help them survive the transplant.

When you purchase a dormant peony division, you'll get a rooted crown with several firm, plump, dark red "eyes," or growth buds, located around it. After planting, one stem should sprout from each eye. Most nurseries sell three- to five-eyed divisions, which should grow to a substantial size a season or two sooner than those with fewer eyes. In either case, you won't get a full complement of blooms until about three years after planting, though some flowers usually form the first year.

Soil preparation and planting—Over the years, I have improved my compacted clay with compost and farmyard manure, transforming it into beautiful, friable loam, full of earthworms and other beneficial denizens of the soil. Even so, I still enrich the soil before planting. To do this, I dig a hole the depth of a shovel blade and wider than the plant's crown. Then I place a small amount of homemade compost in the bottom of the hole, refill it with the soil just dug out, and mix in a couple of handfuls of bone meal. I raise the planting area slightly so that water from melting snow runs away from the crown. This is especially important in our climate, where perennials are more often killed by soggy, wet ground in the spring than by severe winter cold. Then I gently firm the soil to settle it, and fork up the top few inches to create a crumbly planting medium.

To plant, I scoop out some soil, set the divisions with the eyes pointing up, and cover the crown and eyes with no more than 1 in. to 2 in. of soil. (Planting too deep is the most frequent reason why peonies fail to bloom.) I set mine at least 3½ ft. apart.

Since the soil here remains frozen from about mid-November until early April, plants survive much better than in climates where the soil fluctuates between frozen and thawed. If you garden in such an area, you can moderate soil temperatures by mulching the newly-planted divisions with several inches of fluffy, dry material, such as peat moss, and remove it before growth begins in spring.

Peonies in the author's yard include red-flowered 'Louise Van Houtte' and 'Karl Rosenfeld', pink 'Lady Alexandra Duff' (rear) and light pink 'Monsieur Jules Elie' (front).

RESOURCES

For more information about peonies, join the American Peony Society, *250 Interlachen Rd., Hopkins, MN 55343. The annual membership fee ($7.50, individual; $10.00, family) includes four bulletins per year.*

The following mail-order nurseries carry a large selection of herbaceous peonies.

Caprice Farm Nursery, 15425 S.W. Pleasant Hill, Sherwood, OR 97140. 503-625-7241. Catalog $1.00.

Gilbert H. Wild and Son, Inc., P.O. Box 338, Sarcoxie, MO 64862, 417-548-3514. Catalog $3.00.

Honeywood Lilies, Box 63, Parkside, Saskatchewan SOJ 2AO Canada. 306-747-3296 (4/1-10/31) 306-747-3776 (11/1-3/30). Catalog $2.00.

Klehm Nursery, Rt. 5, Box 197, Penny Rd., South Barrington, IL 60010. 800-553-3715. Catalog $4.00.

The New Peony Farm, P.O. Box 18235, St. Paul, MN 55118. Catalog free.

Reath's Nursery, 100 Central Blvd, Vulcan, MI 49892. 906-563-9321. Catalog $1.00.

Tischler Peony Gardens, 1021 East Division St., Faribault, MN, 55021, 507-334-7242. Catalog free.

White Flower Farm, Litchfield, CT 06759. 800-888-7756. Catalog free.

Maintenance

If you want a plant that requires little care, peonies are a good choice. As soon as I can work the ground in the spring, I fork very shallowly around the plants, staying far enough from the center of the crown so I don't spear the fleshy surface roots. Then I top-dress with a shovelful of garden compost and a couple of handfuls of bone meal per plant. These slow-release fertilizers suit my peonies and fit my approach to gardening—I prefer to follow nature's model. Peonies are not excessively heavy feeders, and a diet that's too rich, whether in chemical fertilizers or manure, produces unhealthy plants. Avoid fertilizing with any fresh, wet materials, as they tend to rot the crowns.

Peonies need lots of soil moisture once growth is underway in the spring. When my soil dries out, I trickle-irrigate weekly with about 1 in. of water per plant. In drier climates, start watering in early spring. Continue watering after the plants bloom, as this is the time when the embryonic buds for next year's leaves and flowers are developing. If you overhead water, don't do so when the plants are in bloom. Water landing on already-heavy blooms administers the coup-de-grace, causing them to fall flat on their faces or to break their necks on peony supports.

If you want to get extra large blooms, disbud the plants, removing all of the pea-sized buds along the stem before they swell up, leaving only the uppermost central bud. I prefer to let my peonies run free rather than staking them. Although they sometimes crash to the ground during a heavy rain, I think they look uncomfortable constrained by most supports. Besides, I've yet to find the ideal system. I tried metal peony rings, but after a heavy rain, the upper ring acts as a sort of inverted guillotine, cutting through stems that are bent under the weight of their bloom. I've also placed three or four green bamboo canes around the emerging stems and encircled them with garden twine as the plant grows. This worked better than the rings, but unless I positioned the stakes early in the season, the plants looked as if they were being lassoed or strangled.

My nostalgia will not let the season pass without my cutting some peony blooms for the house. I cut them before the buds open, when they are just starting to show some color and feel soft when gently squeezed. If you set the stems in a vase of water, the flowers will open in a day or so. When the remaining flowers on the plant fade, I deadhead them.

I wait until just before the soil freezes before I cut my peonies to the ground.

You can cut them back around the beginning of August without affecting next year's growth—the plants are dormant by then—but what a pity to miss the autumn foliage colors.

Peonies don't need any mollycoddling over the winter. I think that mulching established plants is generally a waste of time and could even be harmful if you use materials such as hay or leaves, which can become soggy during winter rains or spring snowmelt. To be on the safe side, you could mulch the first winter, especially if you are growing hybrids, which sometimes prove less hardy than the *P. lactiflora* cultivars that I grow.

Few pests and diseases bother peonies; the only disease likely to cause problems is gray mold or botrytis blight (*Botrytis cinerea*). Symptoms of this fungal disease include browning and withering of developing buds and death of the stem beneath, sudden wilting and death of young shoots, blackening and decay of leaves, discoloration at the base of stems and gray-colored mold. To control botrytis, I cut off infected shoots, and if necessary, remove decayed parts of the crown just under the soil surface. Sometimes I dust the plants with powdered sulfur, which serves as a fungicide. I toss all the debris in the garbage—never compost it. As an extra precaution, I replace a little of the soil around infected plants with uncontaminated soil. These cultural practices keep the disease at bay, and I prefer them to the recommended benomyl or captan fungicidal sprays. I have taken an extreme dislike to using any synthetic chemicals, particularly fungicides such as these. Because of their potential toxicity to me and the environment, I cannot justify their use.

In some locations, flower thrips can severely damage opening blooms, causing them to turn brown and fall off. Light-colored, late-blooming double flowers are especially susceptible. To protect the developing buds from thrips, drape spunbonded garden fabric over the buds as soon as they're visible or cut the buds while they are still quite tight and bring them indoors to open.

Pay no attention to the daft notion that you need ants on peony buds to open them. These Epicureans of the insect world are after the sugary nectar the buds exude; they're not some kind of benevolent, fairy flower-openers. Rather than signalling trouble, the presence of ants indicates a healthy bud.

Division

Peonies can be grown from seed, but few home gardeners do so since it takes from four to eight years for plants to bloom from seed, and the hybrids won't come true. The easiest way to increase your peonies is by division, though they don't require it for renewal. You will need a strong spade, a sunny September day, and a willing back. If you haven't already cut back the plants, do so to make them easier to handle. The day before dividing a peony, create a narrow gap between the outer edge of the peony clump and

'Rubra Plena', a double-flowered, old-fashioned cultivar, makes a striking display early in the season.

the surrounding soil by inserting a spade and wiggling it back and forth around the plant. Then leave a hose trickling on the soil for at least half an hour, until the clump is thoroughly moistened. The next day, systematically dig around the plant with a spade, rocking it back and forth until all the roots are cut free. Pry up the clump and pull it out by the stubs of the stems. To make it easier to see what you're doing, knock off as much soil as you can with a strong jet of water.

Leave the clump in the warm sun for an hour or two. This helps soften the roots, making them less susceptible to breaking off. The next step is often daunting to the novice. With the blows of a butcher yet the finesse of a surgeon, sever the tangle of fleshy roots. A quick slice of the spade or drop of the axe will cut the clump up, but this imprecise method can leave some divisions with no eyes. I prefer to divide my peonies with a couple of strong knives and a small saw.

Carefully examine the clump and cut it into pieces, each with three to five eyes and a proportional chunk of roots. Once you make the first division, the rest are usually much easier. Plant the divisions as described earlier. It will probably take them a couple of years to reestablish themselves, but once they do, you'll be rewarded with blooms for years to come. □

David Harrap gardens, writes and appears on a garden radio and TV show in Edmonton, Alberta, Canada.

Nestled among velvety double petals of 'Heritage', a stunning, double, early-blooming peony, this bud of the same cultivar offers the promise of equal beauty.

Hellebores

Perennial magic in the sleeping garden

Hellebores flower at a time when most of the garden is at rest. Despite the late winter snowfalls, the Christmas rose will continue to bloom for a month or more. The handsome, often-evergreen foliage adds texture to shady corners for the remainder of the year.

by Wayne Winterrowd

I know a gardener who always refers to hellebores as "hell-of-a-bores." "What are they, after all?" he asks. "Dull, green-brown, mud-splashed things that always bloom when the garden is looking its worst. Nasty smelling, too, some of them."

To me, however, no large perennial garden—certainly not my own—would be complete without these extraordinary plants. Helle-bores are early-flowering, long-blooming perennials that give color at a time when little else is in flower. Their cup-like flowers, ranging in color from white to plum to pale green and various shades in between, are a welcome sight in my otherwise-desolate March garden here in southern Vermont. And when the blossoms fade, the attractive, finger-like foliage takes over, carpeting shady corners of the garden.

Gardeners in warmer climates will find hellebores even more re-warding. Most species will bloom earlier, and their evergreen leaves, so often scarred and battered by our harsh winters, are more likely to be of year-round interest. Some hellebores are marginally hardy in my USDA Zone 4 garden; one cannot survive the winter at all. But gardeners in Zone 6 to Zone 8 or 9 should have good luck with all of the available varieties, provided the plants are protected from intense sun.

Hellebores belong to the large buttercup family (*Ranunculaceae*), along with such familiar garden plants as anemones, monkshoods and columbines. Their native range runs from the colder parts of Europe to Corsica and southern Greece.

Despite their genetic and geographic diversity, however, all hellebores prefer humus-rich soil and part shade. Though never what you would call stunningly showy in flower, all hellebores have a quiet, subtle beauty that repays looking close, and looking close again. Because of this refinement, I never tire of them in my garden.

It is true that at least one or two species tend towards the malodorous rather than the fragrant, suggesting to many people a scent somewhere between skunk and rancid onion. But the ones that smell this way aren't pushy about it. You have to be given to sniffing out the worst in things to catch their smell at all.

The name *Helleborus* is obscure in origin, dating back to ancient times. I've heard one expert suggest that it derives from the Greek *helein*, to injure, and *bora*, food, which certainly makes sense because all hellebores are poisonous. But I like the vague sense of mystery that hovers around the name "hellebore." It suggests to me dark, evil things, perhaps because the preferred blooming time of many species is around the winter solstice, when most of the things of light are prudently sleeping.

Widely available species

Despite the sinister connotations, the two hellebores most common in gardens have a decided air of sanctity, at least in their common names. They are the Christmas rose (*Helleborus niger*) and the Lenten rose (*H. orientalis*). These are the hellebores with which to start, simply because they are the easiest ones to find. English gardening books describe 20 or so species and many hybrids, some from cold places and all sounding perfectly lovely. But most are unavailable in America as yet, and will probably remain so until hellebores have their vogue.

Christmas rose—The Christmas rose (*Helleborus niger*) is a very hardy perennial (to USDA Zone 3) which grows to 15 in. tall. It has handsome, dark, leathery leaves divided into "palms" of seven leaflets, which are reliably evergreen where winter lows do not dip much below 10°F. The single flowers, borne one, two or three to a stalk, are a warm white, faintly suffused with shell pink and crowded with golden stamens. As with all hellebores, the showy part of the Christmas rose is made up not of petals but of sepals (the petals are present but so small as to attract little notice). The flowers do have the look of certain old roses, such as eglantine, or sweetbrier.

Christmas roses are said, in some more favored climates at least, to bloom reliably at Christmas. I would give much for such a "rose" at Christmas, or for anything else in bloom in my cold, Vermont garden in the dead of winter. Gardeners in warmer regions may see flowers dur-

---

Hellebore (*Helleborus*)

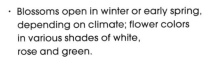

- Perennial with evergreen, finger-like leaves.
- Hardy in USDA Zones 3 to 6, depending on species; most will perform well in warmer climates.
- Blossoms open in winter or early spring, depending on climate; flower colors in various shades of white, rose and green.
- 15 in. to 3 ft. tall.
- Grow in light to deep shade and well-drained, humus-rich soil. Do not allow plants to dry out.
- Plant singly or in small groups as accents, or mass for groundcover effect in dappled woodland or under tall shrubs
- Poisonous

---

ing warm spells as early as December, but for me, the Christmas rose typically blooms in mid-March. It also appears quite naked of its "evergreen" leaves, which do not fare well in our extreme cold. Still, to find a patch of its magical flowers breaking through the snow is to stumble upon a flower as if in a dream, so perfect, pristine and unexpected they are.

Like the flowers of the few other plants that will bloom surrounded by a mantle of crusty snow, the blossoms of the Christmas rose look plucky but entirely vulnerable. Yet, like snowdrops (*Galanthus*) and win-

ter aconites (*Eranthis*), they are actually very tough, seemingly impervious to icy gales or sudden cold snaps. Mud is their only enemy—splashes of it stain their purity. I find that a thick mulch applied in autumn eliminates this problem.

I've been told that, for reasons nobody seems able to explain, the Christmas rose can be difficult to establish. I've never had any such trouble. Even if I had, I wouldn't give up without a fight; the Christmas rose is worth extra effort.

Lenten rose—The Lenten rose, so called because it sometimes blooms in the 40 days before Easter, is not one plant but a large group of related plants offered in catalogs under the name *Helleborus orientalis*. Their leaves are much like those of the Christmas rose, though at maturity they grow 2 in. to 3 in. taller, reaching 18 in. in height. Their nodding flowers appear, several to the stalk, in earliest spring and range in color from greenish white to clear green to green-stained purple. Beautiful forms exist in clear, apple-blossom pink and even in true rose with a deep wine center. But these forms must be vegetatively propagated (a slow process), so they are scarce.

Lenten roses are hardy to Zone 4. For insurance, I place them in the warmest spot in my garden and give them an annual protection of loose spruce boughs in late autumn. The evergreen leaves do get battered by our winters, so I trim them away with shears in early spring before flowering begins, and the new growth quickly fills in.

One of the nicest features of Lenten roses is their generosity with seedlings, which appear beneath the skirts of the mother plants. Lenten roses are a variable group. With a little luck, seedlings may mature into plants with richer flower colors than those you can buy.

Corsican hellebore—Once you've succumbed to the charm of hellebores, you may want to try other species. Only two are readily available in the United States. If I had to choose between them, I would select the Corsican hellebore (*Helleborus lividus corsicus*, also known as *H. argutifolius*), native to that island and to others in the Mediterranean. The Corsican hellebore is a stately perennial, growing to 3 ft. in height.

Its pale green leaves are divided into three leaflets, each dramatically toothed along its margins and netted with veins across its surface.

Lucky gardeners who live in Zone 6 and warmer climates will see it bear its nodding, 2-in.-wide green flowers for more than a month, starting in early spring. To describe them simply as lime or pea green is to do them an injustice, as they are many greens, from pale to dark, overlaid and blended into one another and shading to canary yellow at the center. I've never picked the flowers of the Corsican hellebore because I like them so well where they are, but I can easily imagine how good they would look in a coral pink vase or one of fine old blue porcelain.

I don't grow Corsican hellebores outdoors in my Zone 4 garden, though I intend to try as soon as I have the stock. I have a hunch that the plant might be far hardier than the catalogs say. In the meantime, I've given it a precious 3-sq.-ft. spot of ground in an open bed of my cool (40°F to 50°F) greenhouse. In January my plant covers itself with a green haze of blossoms which last well into May and which are perfect companions to the blooms of the coral and pale pink camellias that grow nearby.

The Corsican hellebore also makes a fine potted plant in a cool greenhouse, though because its nat-

The pale green flowers of the Corsican hellebore (above) have all the freshness of spring. When the 3-ft.-tall flower stalks are cut down, the heavily toothed leaves carry on the show.

ural habit is to flop outward when in flower, like the spokes of a wheel, it requires some staking when grown this way. Even outdoors a little help would be needed to keep the plant upright and looking its best.

Helleborus foetidus—The final hellebore available to American gardeners is *Helleborus foetidus*, native to western Europe. It has two common names: stinking hellebore and bear's foot hellebore. The first name does the plant an injustice. The odor of the flowers is objectionable but very faint; many people don't notice it at all. I don't know the reason for its other common name, but I'd be sorry for the bear who had the misfortune to walk on this plant. In the depths of our winters, its leaves turn as brittle as glass.

The leaves of *Helleborus foetidus* are finely divided into leathery, dark green fingers, seven to ten to a stem. They are handsome in themselves and also a fine and startling accent among other, more predictable, foliage. The flower buds form in late autumn and open to greenish cups rimmed with purple in late March on stalks that grow to 18 in. tall.

This hellebore is said to be hardy only to Zone 6, but I've found it to be much hardier, to Zone 4, if we get our usual snow cover. But when the stems, finely divided leaves and flower buds are turgid with ice, all can be easily snapped off by wind or snow or even by the weight of a bird. To avoid such fracturing, I cover each of my plants carefully with a peach basket.

Should the buds survive the winter to flower in early spring, seed set is abundant. The seedlings appear later in all kinds of unlikely spots in the garden and often thrive where they sprout, requiring, come autumn, yet more peach baskets.

Hellebores in the garden

Although hellebores will accept almost full sun in regions that enjoy really cool summers, in most places the plants perform better in part shade. The high shade of a dappled woodland suits them perfectly, though hellebores will just as happily tuck themselves under the skirts of tall rhododendrons or mountain laurels, as well as deciduous shrubs.

In my garden, I grow hellebores as single plants or in small groups

The green, purple-rimmed flowers of *Helleborus foetidus* (photo middle of page) put on a dramatic display in early spring, but many gardeners grow this plant for its deeply cut leaves. In the woodland setting above, it makes for a distinctive edging, its finger-like foliage contrasting with the more rounded leaf shapes of neighboring plants.

Photos: at top, Jerry Pavia; center and below, Cynthia Woodyard

as accents. But you can also set them out to form a groundcover in a shady corner. Combine the fingered hellebores with broad-leaved plants, such as hostas, for contrast between the two types of foliage. Variegated companions heighten the contrast by bringing light to otherwise-dark sites.

Cultural requirements

The culture of all hellebores is more or less the same. They relish a moist, humus-rich soil that doesn't become waterlogged but that never dries out, either. I mulch heavily with partially decayed leaves or wood chips to preserve soil moisture and keep down weeds. In periods of prolonged drought, I give my plants a thorough soaking every week or so, because a parched soil means certain death. My woodland soil is rich in nutrients, so I don't fertilize my hellebores. For less fertile locations, I would recommend a light sprinkling of a low-nitrogen fertilizer in the spring. I've read that a little lime is also beneficial, probably because most hellebores are native to limestone regions, but as our soil is almost neutral, I've never bothered to add it.

If a new plant adapts well to its site, the first two or three years will see a gratifying increase in the size of the clump, after which it will settle down to more modest enlargement. With luck, within a year or so you'll find single-leaved seedlings clustering beneath the sheltering leaves of mother clumps like chicks beneath a hen. You can leave these seedlings where they sprout to increase the size of your planting, or you can carefully lift them (a kitchen fork is a gentle sort of tool for this work) and transplant them into cool, humusy soil or into pots for eventual placement elsewhere in the garden. Although volunteer seedlings are common around most species, I treasure every seedling because purchased or saved seeds germinate erratically despite great effort on the gardener's part.

Once flourishing, all hellebores should be left for many years without disturbance, which they resent mightily. If you do decide to move or divide a clump, take care when lifting and separating the roots, which are very brittle. English authors recommend doing the work in late August or September. I would

Hellebores can serve as an unusual groundcover in a shaded site. In this Oregon garden, the flowers and dark green foliage of a pale, green-flowered variety of the Lenten rose stand in stunning contrast with the fallen petals of the early-flowering *Rhododendron barbatum*.

SOURCES

The Christmas rose and the Lenten rose are widely available from mail-order nurseries with a large selection of perennials. The following sources also carry, in addition to these plants, the other two hellebores described by the author.

Carroll Gardens, 444 East Main Street, P.O. Box 310, Westminster, MD 21157, 301-848-5422. (*Helleborus foetidus* available by request.) Catalog $2, deductible from first order.

Forestfarm, 990 Tetherow Rd., Williams, OR 97544, 503-846-6963. Catalog $3.

Gossler Farms Nursery, 1200 Weaver Rd., Springfield, OR 97478, 503-746-3922. Catalog $1.

Greer Gardens, 1280 Goodpasture Island Rd., Eugene, OR 97401, 503-686-8266. Catalog $3.

Little River Farm Perennial Nursery, Route 1, Box 220, Middlesex, NC 27557, 919-965-9507. Catalog $2.

Montrose Nursery, P.O. Box 957, Hillsborough, NC 27278, 919-732-7787. Catalog $2.

never dare to do this in my Zone 4 garden, for fear that the alternate freezing and thawing of winter would heave out of the ground plants that had not yet become established. Instead, I handle my hellebores in early spring, usually in early April, and sometimes just as the flowers are passing.

Although hellebores may take two or three years to recover fully after going under the knife, I've never had serious post-operative trouble with divisions. Plants moved all of a piece, however, often sulk and languish, never attaining the vigor they possessed before I relocated them. For this reason, I always divide a clump and plant it as separate pieces rather than moving it as a single plant.

As you would with all other long-lived perennials that are to remain in place undisturbed for a number of years, enrich new planting sites with ample quantities of peat, well-rotted manure or compost. Since hellebores are fussier than most perennials in settling down to a new home, don't take any shortcuts in soil preparation. And be prepared to wait a year or two, or even three, before your plant hits its stride and flowers as you expect. You won't be sorry. □

Wayne Winterrowd is a landscape designer in southern Vermont.

Astilbes are an easy-to-grow, graceful perennial that can provide bloom from early summer through September. At left, planted by author Smith next to an edging of red and white impatiens, the red, plumelike flowers of *Astilbe japonica* 'Bremen' (available from sources 2,3 on p. 38) rise above the delicate, toothed foliage. Above, a dwarf variety of astilbe, *A. chinensis* 'Pumila' (1,2,3,4,5), grows only 10 in. tall and creates a lovely ground-cover edging alongside a walk. In Smith's garden, it blooms during the month of August.

Smith's garden is a burst of color in July, when astilbes and lilies bloom together. Interplanted with the lilies, the astilbes provide shade for the lily roots. The large clump of astilbes shown here is *A.* × *Arendsii* 'Rhineland' (2,3).

Astilbes

Feathery flowers and ferny foliage for moist spots

by John Smith

Astilbes are among the most beautiful, most rewarding and easiest to grow of all herbaceous perennials. From the time they leaf out in early spring until fall frost, their medium- to deep-green, sometimes bronze-red compound leaves, which grow 12 in. to 15 in. tall, complement the other perennials in my garden.

Individual astilbe flowers are tiny, but together they form a striking plumelike inflorescence, called a panicle. This flower stalk, which ranges in height from about 8 in. to nearly 2 ft. depending on the species or cultivar, is rigid and upright, never losing its regal bearing even in heavy wind or rain. In midsummer, when the earliest astilbes flower, the panicles rise above the leaves, richly colored in shades of red, magenta, pink, salmon or creamy white. Each plant bears many panicles—I've counted 12 to 15 on some of my three-year-old plants. Whether planted singly, massed in a border, or combined with other perennials or shrubs, astilbes add a delicate, graceful look to the garden during the entire growing season.

In the garden

Astilbes can be grown throughout much of the United States. Here in southwestern Michigan, they normally bloom in early July. In years when spring comes early, however, some of my astilbes make a show as early as June 5, and peak from mid- to late June. Each species or hybrid blooms for about a month, and by planting successively blooming ones, I can enjoy astilbe flowers through September. If you live in a more southerly state than I do, the bloom time will, of course, be progressively earlier.

Although I grow nearly 150 astilbe plants, I've found attractive ways to combine them with other flowers in my garden—in perennial beds bordering my lawn, under trees, and as focal points around the yard. The blooms of several thousand tulips are a welcome sight in my spring garden, but when their foliage dies back in mid-May, it's quite unsightly. To camouflage the dying leaves, I've planted astilbes among the tulips. Just about the time the tulip foliage begins to mature, the astilbes have leafed out. The two grow quite compatibly side by side—I suspect that some of their roots are intertwined, but the tulip foliage has no trouble pushing its way up in the spring. I also interplant astilbes to disguise the senescent foliage of other bulbs, like scillas and snowdrops, as well as that of spring wildflowers.

Astilbes are the perfect plant to grow in close association with bearded irises, which are the center of attention in my garden at the end of May and early June. Just as the irises finish blooming, the astilbes come on strong, brightening up an area of the garden that would otherwise look drab all summer.

I also mix astilbes in with the more than 200 varieties of lilies I grow. Once again, the astilbe foliage performs a valuable function, providing welcome shade for the lily roots, which prefer a cool place to grow. And the bloom time of the astilbes and lilies overlaps, creating a spectacular and complementary blend of color and form.

Gardeners have a wide choice of astilbes. About four species and numerous hybrids are commercially available; many of the hybrids were developed in the first half of the 20th century in Germany. Because my garden is small, I limit my astilbes to medium-size species and varieties, ones that grow to a total height of no more than 2½ ft. Some of my favorite astilbes are the dwarf varieties, *A. chinensis* 'Pumila', *A. chinensis* 'Finale' and *A. simplicifolia* 'Sprite'. (All are available from sources 1,2,3,4,5 listed on p. 38.) Growing only 8 in. to 15 in. tall, they're ideal for the front of borders, in rock gardens and as ground covers. They're without equal for late-season bloom. Their flowers in shades of pink and lavender provide color in my garden from late August through mid-September. 'Finale' has an especially delicate color—quite a bit of white with just a hint of pink. All three also tolerate deep shade and drier conditions than the *A. × Arendsii* hybrids do.

But hybrids of *A. × Arendsii* figure prominently in my garden as well. Though the first plants I received 20 years ago from a friend in the Netherlands weren't labeled, I think two of them are 'Federsee' (2,3,5), whose flowers are carmine-rose with a hint of salmon, and 'Fanal' (1,2,3,4,5), a bronze-leaved plant with dark-red blooms. Even if the plants had been labeled, I couldn't count on the names being totally accurate. Commercially available cultivars are sometimes misnamed, so two with the same name from two different sources may vary in color. Fortunately, a committee of those involved in the astilbe trade are trying to clear up the confusion.

Over the years, I've grown many of the creamy-white-flowered species and cultivars, but I've gotten rid of most of them. They don't grow as vigorously in my garden as the pink- and red-flowered ones do, and seem to require more water. Among the popular white-flowered astilbes are cultivars of *A. Thunbergii*; *A. × Arendsii* hybrids including 'Bridal Veil' (2,3), 'Snowdrift' (2,3,5) and 'Irrlicht' (1,2,3); and *A. japonica* 'Deutchland' (1,2,3,4).

Though I've never grown them, I've seen several taller varieties, all reaching 3 ft. to 4 ft., which would make excellent background plants for a large perennial garden: *A. × Arendsii* 'Cattleya', with rose-pink flowers (1,2,3,4,5); 'Ostrich Plume', with coral-pink flowers (1,2,3,4); and *A. taquetii* 'Superba', with purple-rose flowers (1,2,3,4).

Growing astilbes

Hardiness—The cultivated astilbes are hardy from USDA Zone 4 (to -30°F) through Zone 8 (to 10°F), reflecting their native habitat. They're dependably hardy here in Michigan, in Zone 5. An unusually late frost last spring killed back the new foliage, but it regrew and the plants flowered just fine, though they bloomed later than usual. North of here, I wouldn't count on astilbes surviving the winters. In southern states, astilbes are hardy, but growing them is more difficult because they seem unable to stand a steady diet of intense heat, particularly hot afternoon sun. Yet if they're given plenty of water, and in some climates afternoon shade, I'm convinced that astilbes can be successfully grown in the South.

Watering—Water is the key to successful astilbe growing. Astilbes require a constant supply of moisture throughout the growing season. In periods of hot, drying winds and little rainfall, and just before and during bloom, irrigation is vital. Astilbes will let you know quickly if they're not getting enough moisture—their leaves curl up, their flower plumes droop and the entire plant looks downright pathetic. Fortunately, they revive if they're generously watered right away. During the extremely hot summer of 1988, temperatures in my garden reached into the 90s, but with ample irrigation, my astilbes thrived.

The precise amount of water depends, of course, on your site conditions and climate—factors such as soil type, amount of rainfall, time of year, and exposure to sun and wind, to name a few. My garden soil is rapidly draining gravel fill about 2 ft. deep. During summer dry spells, I routinely soak the back and side gardens every other day, using an in-ground sprinkler system. In the front yard, two big trees seem to pull all the water out of the soil, so I often have to sprinkle the astilbes there daily to keep them from drooping.

In contrast, friends of mine who garden in clay soil irrigate their astilbes much less frequently than I do. I've also seen naturalized plantings of astilbes growing beautifully without any irrigation in low-lying areas bordering a pond or creek where the soil remains damp. In the end, the best advice I can give is to make sure your astilbes are constantly moist.

Site selection—Most nursery catalogs would have you believe that astilbes do best in shady conditions. Knowing the difficulty of raising astilbes in the South, where they're likely to dry out in the hot sun, this recommendation makes some sense. In my garden, however, astilbes perform poorly in full shade. They will bloom, but the plants and flowers won't be nearly as large or as vigorous as those planted in full sun or partial shade.

I've had the best results with astilbes planted in full sun, as long as I make sure the soil is moist at all times and the air circulation is good. I avoid planting them close to a solid wood fence or wall, or against the south- or west-facing foundation of my house—reflected light from these surfaces bakes the plants and air doesn't circulate well.

A clump of *A. × Arendsii* 'Irrlicht' (1,2,3), about 2 ft. tall, blooms in July in Smith's garden. He rarely grows creamy-white-flowered astilbes, since they don't grow as vigorously in his garden as the red- or pink-flowered ones do.

Semi-shady locations are the next best exposure. Astilbes do well along the north and east sides of my house, and in the shadow of—not directly beneath—bushes and trees. They do fine in the shade cast by my house, the fence and trees, as long as sunlight isn't obstructed from overhead.

Soil preparation and planting—I've found that astilbes *must* be grown in soil enriched with organic matter, both for the nutrients it provides and for its water-holding capabilities. Since my gravel soil was so devoid of organic matter, I had to add some, but even more humusy soils would benefit from amendment. Over the past 20 years, I've improved my soil by mulching with shredded leaves—a free and abundant material in my area. I'm sure other organic materials, such as peat moss, rotted manure, grass clippings, compost or shredded bark, would work as well. In the fall, I spread a layer of shredded leaves, 1½ in. to 2 in. deep, on all my flower beds. The leaves stay put throughout the winter and protect and enrich the soil until early July; by then they've been almost entirely digested by worms and microorganisms and converted into rich soil. At that time, I lightly mulch with grass clippings or leaf mold. Over the years, the mulch has enriched my soil so much that I no longer need to add any other fertilizers. In a less fertile soil, you might need to apply a balanced, organically based fertilizer formulated for outdoor plants. With the mulch, I irrigate less frequently than before, and I no longer have to endure the drudgery of weeding. During a rainfall, it protects the flowers

Given plenty of moisture and a soil rich in organic matter, Smith's astilbes thrive in full sun. Here, the red flowers of *A. × Arendsii* 'Federsee' (2,3,5) and the pink ones of an unnamed seedling complement the foliage of Japanese painted ferns and disguise the spent foliage of early-blooming bulbs and wildflowers.

SOURCES

1. **André Viette Farm and Nursery**, Rt. 1, Box 16, Fishersville, VA 22939. 703-943-2315. Catalog $2.00.

2. **Busse Gardens**, Rt. 2, Box 238, Cokato, MN 55321. 612-286-2654. Catalog $2.00.

3. **Carroll Gardens**, P.O. Box 310, Westminster, MD 21157. Catalog $2.00.

4. **Milaeger's Gardens**, 4838 Douglas Ave., Racine, WI 53402. 414-639-2371. Catalog $1.00. $25.00 minimum order.

5. **Wayside Gardens**, Garden Lane, Hodges, SC 29695. 800-845-1124. Catalog free.

The rich red blooms of *A. × Arendsii* 'Fanal' (1,2,3,4,5), blooming in July, nestle among iris foliage. The arendsii hybrids are probably the most commonly available astilbes.

from splashing mud. Year-round, the mulch gives the garden a tidy, attractive look.

I purchase my astilbes in the spring from mail-order nurseries, either container-grown or bare-root. (Local garden centers stock astilbes, but often don't indicate the variety.) I transplant container-grown astilbes much the same as I would any other perennial: I gently tap each plant out of the pot, rough up the edges of the root ball to loosen any pot-bound roots, plant it with the crown at the soil surface and water it in well. I usually space the plants about 2 ft. apart to allow plenty of room for them to grow.

Maintenance—Other than needing mulching and watering, astilbes are a carefree plant. During their bloom time, I often cut the fresh flowers, which look elegant in arrangements. After flowering is completed, some gardeners just leave the flower stalks in place—they're reasonably attractive even after the color fades. I prefer to remove the stalks after bloom, cutting them off well below the foliage. By doing so, the flowers don't detract from those of nearby perennials, while the leaves remain as a lovely ferny accent. Some of my friends dry the spent flower stalks, combining them in bouquets with other dried flowers. Dried astilbe flowers are appealing in their natural colors, or even when spray-painted in other colors.

After a killing frost, I cut off the dead foliage nearly to the ground, leaving no more than ½ in. of leaf stalks to mark each plant's location. I learned the value of this practice shortly after my first venture with astilbes. At that time, I made the mistake of leaving the foliage in place over the winter. Some sucking insect made a snug winter home in it, and then rewarded me the following summer by disfiguring the foliage with a myriad of small holes. Since then, I've always cut away all the foliage and relegated it to the trashcan—and I've never had a pest (or a disease) problem since.

Division—Astilbes grow rapidly. A plant purchased in a 4-in. or 6-in. pot will expand in the garden to a sizable clump, 10 in. to 12 in. in diameter, within three years. Some of my plants have grown even larger. Sometime between the third and fifth year in the garden, large clumps lose some of their flowering vigor. To renew them, I divide the plants every three years, or when they've reached roughly 1 ft. in diameter. (Astilbes will self-seed, and in my garden, volunteers flower after about three years. The flower color and form of the plants vary slightly from that of the parents.)

Fall is the best time to divide astilbes. I generally do it around mid- to late September, which gives the new transplants plenty of time to establish themselves before winter sets in. It's easiest to get an idea of the size of the clump and to dig it out once the foliage is out of the way, so I begin by trimming the foliage close to the ground, just as I do after frost-kill. Then I dig out the clump, slicing the soil a few inches beyond the root ball on all sides. Once I've hefted the clump onto the soil, I use a very sharp, sturdy serrated knife or a flat sharp-edged spade for cutting it apart. The fibrous roots are very densely packed and the root ball tough and difficult to separate, so it normally takes repeated sawing or just jamming the spade through the root ball to cut through it. I divide the clump into quarters, cutting through it from top to bottom. Then I transplant each portion into its new location and water it in thoroughly. Dividing astilbes in the spring would probably work, but I think it would be difficult to do while tussling with the new spring growth.

Like newly transplanted astilbes from the nursery, fall-planted divisions will bloom the following summer.

I hardly view dividing astilbes as a chore. Making lots of new plants has greatly increased my collection, with no out-of-pocket expense. By quartering my first three plants at three-year intervals, I ended up with 48 astilbes in six years. I really got my money's worth. I bartered the extra plants with other gardeners, or with friends who are nurserymen, for other plants I wanted and so built my collection. I've given away hundreds of astilbes to relatives, neighbors, friends and visitors to our garden—they've become infatuated with them, too. ☐

John W. (Jack) Smith gardens in Grand Rapids, Michigan.

The feathery pink blooms of A. × rosea 'Peach Blossom' (1,2,3,5), a July-blooming, 2½-ft.-tall plant, rise above a ground cover of fibrous begonias.

Daylilies

Fleeting flowers are the mainstay of this summer garden

by Sydney Eddison

The essence of the daylily's powerful attraction is captured in its name. Even the most literal-minded daylily grower is stirred by the evanescence of the individual blossoms. Perfect for a day and gone the next, they represent the attainment of youth and beauty with no strings attached and no price to pay later. To grow daylilies is to have your cake and eat it, too.

But, beautiful and addictive as the flowers are, for me the charm of the daylily as a garden plant lies also in its versatility. The flowers offer a palette of colors, forms and sizes, which can be assembled at different heights in a flowing, ever-changing tapestry with other perennials. Multiplying generously but keeping neatly to themselves, daylilies enhance nearby plants without overwhelming them.

These qualities have made daylilies the mainstay of my summer garden. The plants run like a repeated theme throughout the perennial border and reappear, here and there, on the hillside beyond. They brighten alcoves among the rhododendrons, and spotlight either end of a hosta and fern planting as it emerges from the dense shade of an old maple. Recently, I have begun work on a bed that will bind together rocks and shrubs with a pastel ribbon of daylilies.

When I started gardening 25 years ago, daylilies occupied less exalted positions in my garden and in my affections. After a first, and disappointing, attempt to use daylilies as a ground cover in a spot both too shady and too dry, I tried to hold and cover an awful-looking bank with them. The bank, a long heap of rubble and fill, ran north and south along the slope of an existing hillside in our backyard. With a minimum of soil preparation and the casual addition of peat moss, I installed a dozen plants of the old daylily cultivar 'Marionette'.

To my surprise, the plants prospered. In a year, the group, with their golden-yellow flowers, made quite a show of bold color. I also noticed how striking the blossoms looked as they leaned slightly downhill toward the morning sun, each exposed throat showing the full beauty of a contrasting maroon "eye." The gentle incline of the slope accentuated the grace of the plants' wand-like flower stalks and narrow, flowing leaves.

The daylilies flaunting their trumpets from the bank made me aware of hitherto unsuspected possibilities in the sloping site. I decided to abandon the struggle to make a small perennial border in a stretch of flat lawn, and to focus on the bank, with its obstacle course of rocks and trees. This decision launched my gardening career, and I began a lifelong enjoyment of the genus *Hemerocallis*.

Some background—The name *Hemerocallis* was the choice of Carolus Linnaeus, the 18th-century Swedish naturalist whose classification system brought order to the plant world. In Linnaeus's time, only two species of daylily had found their way to Europe from the Orient. Both are familiar to us today: the tawny daylily (*H. fulva*) that lines country roads all across the United States, and the lemon lily (*H. Lilio-asphodelus*, formerly called *H. flava*), an old-fashioned garden favorite with scented yellow flowers that here in the Northeast bloom around Memorial Day. Their flowers, with slender, flaring tepals and modest size, are typical of species daylilies. (Generally, the outer three segments of a daylily flower are referred to as sepals and the inner three as petals. Botanically, all six are tepals.) If Linnaeus admired these two species, he would be awestruck by the appearance of modern daylily hybrids, which come in every size, shape and hue imaginable.

In fact, I've grown daylilies long enough to be awestruck myself by today's hybrids. In 1961, when I first planted them, commercially available daylilies came in far fewer colors and forms. Now it is difficult to even suggest the range of daylily colors. Suffice it to say that the only color that still eludes the hybridizers is blue. Flowers range in size from 1½ in. to as much as 9 in. in diameter, and flower stalks (called scapes) can be as lofty as 6 ft. or as low as 6 in. So great are the variations in modern daylilies that a system categorizing flower size, form and color pattern, and scape height has evolved to help enthusiasts sort them out. A handbook from the American Hemerocallis Society (see Sources, p. 45) provides this and much other useful information.

When the AHS was founded in 1946 to encourage the development of daylilies, it found a receptive audience. Forty years later, there are 275 registered daylily breeders, hundreds more amateur hybridizers, and 29,960 named daylily cultivars.

In fact, so many new cultivars are proposed each year for official naming that some Society members are calling for greater selectivity in their registration. One of the reasons for this explosion is the ease with which daylilies can be crossed to produce new hybrids. Still, only a small number actually make it into commerce; enough, nonetheless, to create problems for people like me who want to try more of them than they have room for.

In the garden

By 1965, the daylilies on my bank had been joined by other perennials, refugees from the bed in the middle of the lawn. Although the slope is well drained, only the daylilies, peonies and some irises

thrived in their rugged new situation and tolerated the benign neglect that was their lot while I worked full time. I was grateful for the daylilies' individual tenacity and their collective usefulness in disguising the rubble. But it wasn't until I sent for a catalog from the daylily specialists, Gilbert H. Wild and Son, Inc. (see Sources), that I became infatuated with the flowers. And, as I acquired more daylilies, I had to figure ways to use them in my ever-expanding garden.

Height—I'd describe my garden today as a rambling, country affair. It is generally viewed from afar, so it takes large, robust plants with plenty of flowers to make an impact. I combine large-flowered daylilies with tall scapes with other stal-

wart perennials of about the same stature, degree of vigor and quantity of bloom for an eye-catching effect. In one spot in the border, for example, a mass of 'Painted Lady', about 3 ft. high, shows off its widely spread, clear, light-orange blossoms against the great yellow bells of *Lilium* 'Golden Splendor'; a single plant of the prickly-headed globe thistle, *Echinops Ritro*; and the narrow but numerous spikes of *Lythrum* 'Dropmore Purple'.

Tall daylilies with small flowers also

In July and August, daylilies dominate Eddison's gently sloped perennial border (above). Yellow, orange and red varieties repeat throughout at various heights, and in combination with flowers of similar or strikingly different color.

Maroon markings on the petals of an old bicolor daylily (center), whose name is unknown to Eddison, are picked up with a vengeance by the red of 'Shining Plumage' (right). The silvery blue balls of globe thistle provide contrast in color and form.

Eddison combines colorful daylilies with light-blue flax (foreground), electric-blue globe thistle and *Lilium* 'Golden Splendor'. Carried high on thin stalks, the daylily flowers don't obscure the plants behind them. The red and gold bicolor daylily is 'Bright Banner', the yellow and red bicolor is an old cultivar whose name is unknown to Eddison, and the red daylily is 'Shining Plumage'.

have their uses. I have a group of six-footers, 'Autumn Minaret', planted high on the slope behind the perennial border, where their relatively small yellow flowers seem to be floating among the deep-green leaves of the rhododendrons. The low foliage and long, bare stems of the daylilies are concealed behind the broad-leaf evergreens.

Miniature daylilies have flowers less than 3 in. in diameter and foliage that is comparable in scale. They are valuable in a mass planting where they can be used almost like a ground cover. I'm working on a planting that surrounds a recently acquired rhododendron with miniature cultivars, such as 'Robin Coleman', a neat little golden-flowered plant. At the other extreme, the giant 'Yellow Pinwheel', with tall stalks as thick as a man's thumb and eye-catching flowers 8 in. across, is best used as a single accent plant. I have it at the back of the border, where its rather clumsy scapes disappear against the foliage of even taller sunflowers.

Perennial borders planted in carefully graduated heights look too planned and military for my taste. Instead, I prefer to break up the solid mass of plants in the middle of the border with sudden spurts of height. Daylilies with scapes that rise far above their foliage, such as 'Purity', are ideal for this purpose. The flowers seem to hover above the garden, while their thin scapes blend into the background without obstructing the viewer's enjoyment of somewhat shorter plants behind them. I also use daylilies of moderate heights right in front of the border. I've planted 'Sparks', for example, which carries its brilliant red-orange flowers

well above the leaves, next to slightly shorter yarrow, whose flat yellow flower clusters are clearly visible through the daylily scapes.

Bloom—Among the qualities that make daylilies invaluable in the perennial border are the profusion of flowers and their long season of bloom. Although the individual flowers are poignantly short-lived, a single plant can produce a great many. I've read that a single, well-branched scape can produce up to 100 buds, but I'm pleased with cultivars like 'Echo Valley', which produces three dozen or so blossoms to a scape. In a nice big clump with ten scapes, that makes 360 flowers. Not bad for one plant!

While peonies are a nine-day wonder and bearded irises may last a week, four weeks of bloom is not uncommon among daylilies. Although most of my daylilies flower in July and early August, I've found some that will stretch the season from May to October. There are also re-bloomers, cultivars that flower in their proper season, then again later. In the Northeast, a second flush of bloom is not common, but I'm going to try 'Stella d'Oro', a low-growing miniature with beautifully wrought flowers, on the recommendation of friends here who get scape after scape all season long from it.

Foliage—Since most perennials seldom flower for longer than two weeks, foliage is also an important consideration in a mixed border. Daylily leaves are attractive through much, though not all, of the season. Folded lengthwise and overlapping at the base, daylily leaves emerge in pairs from an underground stem. As the leaves lengthen out, they loosen their embrace and spread open like a fan, soon making a handsome fountain-like clump of foliage. Fans of medium-sized daylilies at the front of my border appear about the middle of April, and within a month, they conceal the yellowing leaves of daffodils and tulips. Then, for a time, sprays of arching daylily leaves fill in gaps between peonies and irises, contrasting pleasantly in form and color with the broad, divided peony foliage and erect iris blades. During the daylilies' star turn, the foliage makes a green backdrop for their own and other flowers.

There are three classifications of daylily foliage: deciduous, evergreen and semi-evergreen. These are based on the response of the plant's leaves to the changing seasons and do not necessarily denote hardiness. At least some varieties in all three classes can be grown in cold climates. I grow deciduous daylilies, and have to admit that after the plants have flowered, their foliage goes into a decline. Considering all the pleasure the plants have given me by then, I'm willing to live with some brown foliage. A new flush of growth in the early fall produces fresh green leaves. Then after repeated hard freezes, all the leaves die down, and I remove them to reduce the chances of har boring pests and diseases during the winter.

I don't grow evergreen daylilies, whose foliage stays green all winter, no matter how cold the weather gets, or semi-evergreen daylilies, the ends of whose leaves brown during the winter. I'm concerned that our winter cycles of freeze and thaw would rot the leaves and the rot would extend underground and damage the plants. Of course, winter care can affect a plant's behavior. I recently visited a magnificent daylily garden in New York State where all three classes overwinter just fine under a mulch of salt hay 8 in. deep.

Combinations—The subtle variations in the form and shape of daylily flowers are really lost in a garden the size of mine. They can best be admired at close range or in a special place where one can marvel at the ingenuity of hybridizers and compare the barely perceptible differences in configuration. The same is true of the subtlest pastel colors. Lovely in themselves, they demand settings that permit close attention. I have a pearly cream and pink polychrome called 'Satin Glass'. Set among the lavender bell-hung spires of hosta in the shade of a maple tree, the broad-faced flowers have a radiant, ghostly quality.

This pastel combination is a knockout, but it's one of the few such color arrangements in my garden. Mine is not a cool, misty, English-style garden of blues, lavenders, pinks and pale yellows. I happen to love yellow, and not necessarily pale yellow. So mine is a hot garden of sunny col-

Often overlooked because of the plant's spectacular flowers, daylily foliage has its own attractions and uses. The foliage of the buff-colored daylily 'Varsity' contrasts nicely in form and color with that of the sedum 'Autumn Joy' to its right and the foliage of *Iris lactea* beneath it. The attractive tangle also covers a hole in the garden left by earlier-blooming bulbs.

ors—golds, shades of orange from brick to copper to apricot, and, at the far end of the span, a warm buff color. Quite a few shades of red combine well with yellow and orange, but I discovered that blue-reds are intrusive and that true blues don't work either. One exception is a spatter-dash of sky-blue flax (*Linum perenne*) sprinkled against the background of large, colorful daylilies—orange-red 'Sparks', brick and gold 'Bright Banner', and rich red 'Shining Plumage' (bottom photo, facing page).

One other blue flower is extremely successful among the warm colors and flaring shapes of the daylily blossoms: globe thistle. The dozens of tiny individual flowers in the ball-shaped flower head seem to absorb light, in marked contrast to the broad, light-reflecting segments of the daylilies. The undemanding shade of

blue-gray rests the eye and points up the brilliance of other nearby flowers. I've planted four large clumps of globe thistle at intervals throughout the border.

Repetition helps to order things for a viewer, which can be reassuring when there's a lot going on in the garden. In several places in the border, I've planted groups of daylilies in a pleasant shade of muted coral. Early in the season comes 'Sweetbriar', an old-fashioned cultivar. Its coral flowers are a wonderful binder and go well with lemon-yellow 'Hyperion' (a daylily cultivar I've also repeat-planted) and with the globe thistle. Later, 'Candy', a daylily in the same shade of muted coral, picks up where 'Sweetbriar' leaves off, blooming with the warm-yellow 'Purity' and repeating the yellow/coral theme.

I would feel like a complete fraud if I

Parent
Leaf fan

Leaf scars

*New crowns, flower scapes
and rhizomes can develop
from axillary buds nestled
between leaf scars.*

Crown
(modified
stem)

Roots

Offspring

*Swollen root segments
store water.*

Daylilies underground
by Gregory Piotrowski

Though daylilies are members of the lily
family, Liliaceae, they are easily distinguished
from true lilies by several characteristics. The
most obvious difference is that lilies grow from
a bulb, while daylilies grow from a fleshy
rootstock. This rootstock consists of a dense
root system attached to a compact, modified
stem (called a crown) situated near the soil
surface.

You can think of a daylily crown as a
branching system, just like that of a tree or a
shrub, in which new stems arise from older
ones. All of the tissues of a typical stem—leaf
nodes, axillary or lateral buds and
internodes—are there, but are compressed
like an accordian. Look closely at a daylily
crown when you transplant one. The rings are
leaf scars, each a node where a leaf once
grew. Between the rings, so tightly packed as
to be practically nonexistent, are the
internodes. Above each scar is an axillary
bud, which can develop into a new crown, a
flower scape or a rhizome (in certain
daylilies), or it may not develop at all. Exactly
what causes a developing axillary bud to
become a flower scape instead of a crown,
for example, is uncertain.

New crowns form on top of older ones,
and can create a clump or hummock. Over
time, the mass of crowns slowly becomes
shallower in the soil, even though the roots are
trying to pull the plant down. With many stems
competing in the same space for moisture
and nutrients, growth is weak, so such clumps
need to be divided to maintain the vigor of
the plants.

The common tawny daylily, *Hemerocallis
fulva*, and several other daylilies have another
type of modified stem called a rhizome.
Rhizomes grow horizontally just beneath the
soil surface and can grow to more than 1 ft. in
length, producing a new plant at the growing
tip. Because all of the rhizomes grow from a
single parent, the whole colony is one plant.
The tawny daylily produces no fertile seed,
but the rhizomes are segmented and can be
broken apart easily without being severed. It
is by division of these colonies, either by man
or by nature, that this plant has been widely
dispersed. Daylilies that produce rhizomes
seem to increase at a quicker rate and
spread much faster than do the clump-
forming types. □

*Gregory Piotrowski is a gardener at the New
York Botanical Garden.*

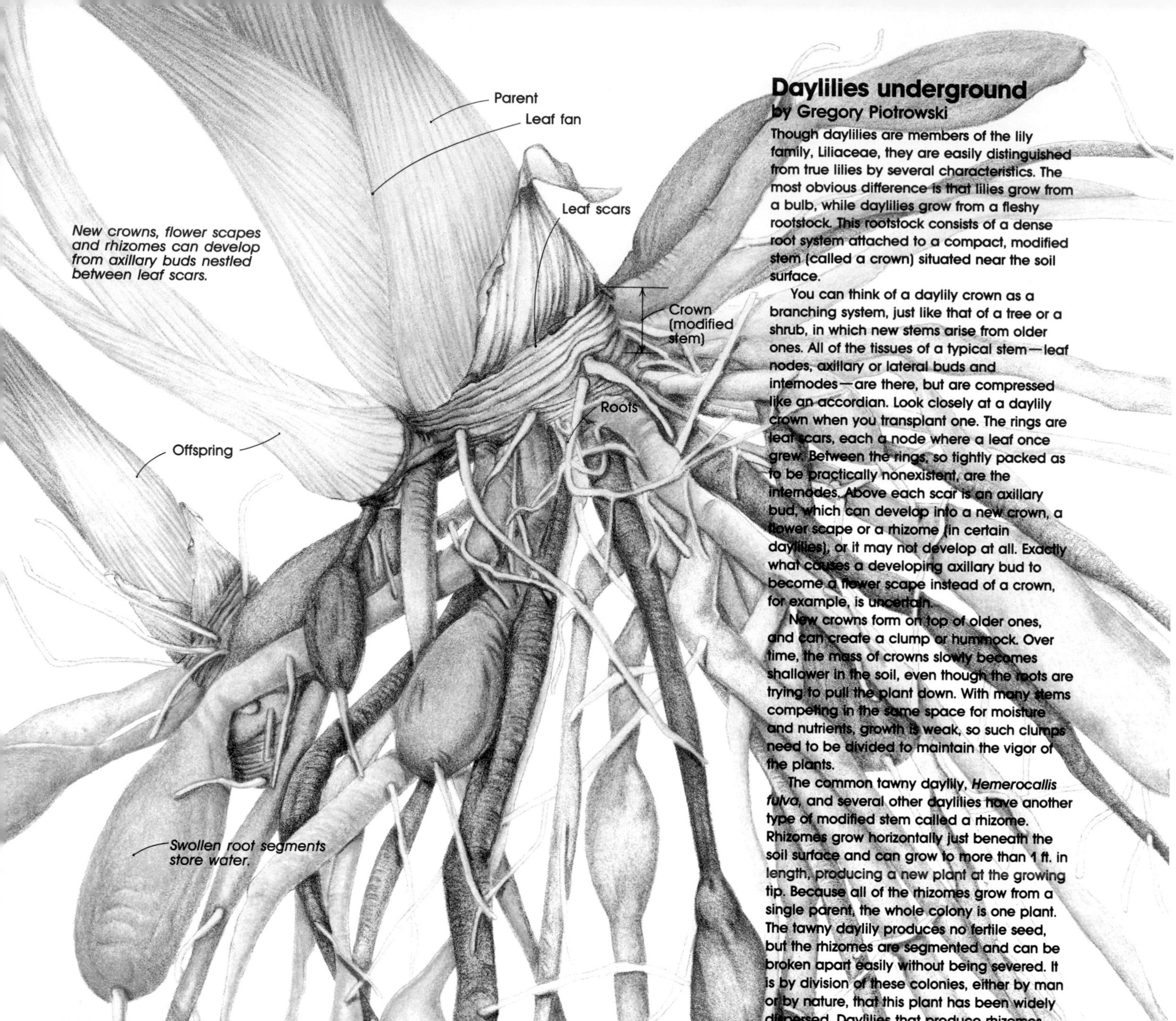

Even very large old clumps of daylilies can be divided by hand, though it takes some energy, as
Eddison demonstrates here. A single clump (far
left) yields many. Larger divisions will make a
show sooner, but smaller ones won't need dividing as soon.

Drawing: Rosalind Loeb Wanke

didn't admit that the color scheme and plant combinations described here evolved over 20-odd years. They are the product of constant tinkering rather than careful analysis, and the choices reflect both the intentional and the expedient. Sometimes I'm painfully aware that the design will suffer from the inclusion of a new acquisition, but the newcomer goes in anyway. Daylilies present a particularly knotty problem for the compulsive plant collector—there's always a new one you want. That means that an old one ought to go. But if I'm fond of the old one, they both stay.

Propagation

Hybrid daylilies don't reproduce true from seed, so when you buy a named variety, you buy a plant that's been reproduced vegetatively, usually by division. (See facing page for more on how daylilies reproduce.) Once you've bought a variety, division will allow you to spread it around the garden. Division also maintains the vigor of a clump. Meticulous daylily growers divide every three years, but I divide when a clump seems to be flowering less profusely, which can take quite a few years. I'm ashamed to say that there are clumps of daylilies in my garden that haven't been divided in 20 years. Division would improve them, but they still bloom faithfully.

The technique for dividing daylilies couldn't be simpler, though strenuous for overgrown clumps. Daylilies can be divided at any time of year, but I find it easiest during the resting period that follows flowering, since many of the outer leaves turn brown and can be pulled off, and the rest of the foliage can be cut down to 8 in. to 10 in. First, I dig up the whole mass with a strong garden fork. An overgrown clump of daylilies with a great wad of roots, hopelessly intertwined and covered with dirt, is a daunting sight. So I wash off as much earth as possible, then commence pulling this mass apart into smaller clusters of roots and foliage.

To achieve this end, pretty much anything goes. Sometimes I can shake, wiggle and tease the clump apart. But if the mass of roots is impenetrable, I resort to sawing through the clump, using a heavy knife with a serrated blade. This drastic maneuver severs roots, but there are so many in a large clump that it doesn't matter. When the prospect of lifting and sawing apart a very large old clump of daylilies has been too off-putting, I've taken a sharp spade and dug chunks off the outside of the clump. In the holes left behind, I put rotted manure or compost, which does seem to revitalize the remaining daylilies.

Unless you want to get as many single plants as possible from a clump, the divisions can be as large or as small as needed. Obviously, smaller clumps will take longer to make a show; larger ones will need dividing sooner. I haven't tried it, but dividing into small clumps and planting a group of them together makes sense: You'll get a nice display quickly, the clumps will have optimum elbow room for proper development, and division will be easier the next time.

I try to plant newly divided and newly arrived daylilies as soon as possible so that they won't dry out. Divisions and new arrivals can withstand considerable delay in planting, however, if they are kept moist and shaded. Water loss from either the roots or the foliage is to be avoided. Clumps with earth left around their roots can be stored in plastic bags rolled down to expose the foliage to the air. I've also kept bare-root divisions in buckets with a little water in the bottom for as long as a week (the water should be changed daily).

Planting is straightforward. I spread the roots over the bottom of a generous hole, positioning the crown about the same depth as it was before division and filling in with soil. (If placed more than an inch deeper, the crown may not grow or flower properly.) A good soaking finishes the job. Although it's always best to plant in the cool of the day, once in the ground, daylilies are so tolerant that no special precautions—such as further shading—are required.

Cultivation and maintenance

I learned the hard way that my garden is no place for imperious, aristocratic plants that demand special care and attention. So now I grow only easy, broad-minded perennials that share accommodations and receive similar treatment. The gentle slope of my perennial border provides good drainage, and woodland to the north and west shelters the plantings from the prevailing winds. Daylilies need at least six hours of sun a day; my border is in full sun from early morning until mid-afternoon. The border's only problem has always been its poor, rocky soil. Though daylilies will grow in almost any kind of soil, they're healthier and produce more flowers in soil rich in organic matter.

Because the border grew by increments—about 50 sq. ft. a year—some sections have better soil than do others. As I became a better gardener, I took more trouble to prepare a new section of bed properly by digging as deeply as possible and adding as much peat moss, compost, manure and old hay as I could. At its best, the soil is fairly open and has quite a bit of humus, which I think is more important than any other single thing in growing happy plants.

I fertilize the whole border once a year in the spring. Around each plant, I scatter and lightly scratch in a small handful of 10-10-10 commercial fertilizer. And for the last few years I've maintained a summer mulch of shredded leaves about 3 in. deep. I swear by this mulch, and I know it has improved the soil by retaining moisture and eventually breaking down to add humus.

Good soil preparation, a sprinkling of fertilizer and the application of mulch are as much as I can do for the daylilies and other perennials I grow. And that's all they seem to demand. The daylilies would appreciate a good soaking rain once a week early in the season—drought retards the formation of the flower buds. But our well isn't up to watering the garden, and even if nature doesn't provide, the plants still get along.

Daylilies seem to have fewer insect enemies than do some of my other perennials. With the exception of a single daylily cultivar, 'Wee Willie Winkie', which repeatedly attracted the cyclamen mite, I've encountered few problems. Occasionally, a few of the dark-colored daylily flowers will be disfigured by a light-colored, irregular track on the petals that's caused by thrips. The American Hemerocallis Society's handbook warns, "If you have never sprayed and have had little damage, do NOT begin a program of spraying." I've taken this advice to heart and refrained from spraying. □

Sydney Eddison is a contributing editor to Fine Gardening.

Veronicas

Adaptable perennials bloom in vivid blues

by Panayoti Kelaidis

I've never met a gardener who didn't love blue flowers. Nothing attracts livelier debate in gardening circles than color, but everyone agrees on one point—there's never enough blue. Gardeners take great pains to stake up their tall, blue delphiniums or to fuss over blue gentians; breeders dream of creating blue roses and blue dahlias. Meanwhile, veronicas effortlessly carpet the garden year after year with rich, blue-violet flowers. Maybe it's time to give veronicas their due.

Veronicas grow with much the same gusto in California gardens as they do in the upper Midwest or deep in the southeastern coastal belt. I've found few perennials that have a wider tolerance for different soils and extremes of climate and moisture. And few perennials live so long, are as easy to grow, or have as few pest and disease problems as veronicas do. As a gardener who has worked for over a decade coddling delicate alpine plants in a public garden, I have gained increasing respect for plants like veronicas that don't need frequent rejuvenation or replacement.

Commonly known as speedwells, veronicas are members of the figwort family, along with foxgloves, penstemons and mullein. Between 200 and 300 species of veronica have been identified, growing on every continent except Antarctica. They live in deserts,

The bright blue flowers of spike veronica 'Blue Fox' offer a color that is welcome in any garden. Like other veronicas, this 15-in. tall cultivar tolerates an amazingly wide range of growing conditions compared to most other perennials.

Veronica (*Veronica*)
ve-RON-i-kah

- Perennial, 1 in. to 18 in. tall.
- Blue, blue-violet, pink or white flowers, depending on species or cultivar.
- Prefers full sun; tolerates wide range of soils and moisture.
- Widely-adapted, hardy to USDA Zone 3.
- Well-suited for planting in a flower border or rock garden, or as a ground cover.

on tundra, in water, in woods and meadows, and even in the tiniest crevices of solid rock. Given that, it's no surprise that one or another speedwell is sure to thrive in almost any microclimate your garden can provide.

Most veronicas have blue-violet flowers; a few come in shades of pastel blue, pink or even white. Their blossoms open on spires ranging from an inch to nearly one foot in length. The individual blossoms are usually small, rarely reaching ½ in. across, and consist of four petals often marked with dark lines. All veronicas have a long season of showy bloom—some species open in early spring, while a few bloom in late summer. Most veronicas have medium green, finely textured evergreen foliage, which gives the plants year-round appeal.

The most commonly cultivated veronicas are low-growing species, perfect for the fronts of borders or as small-scale ground covers. Lesser-known species include taller veronicas often used in flower borders and ground-hugging cushions or mats that look best planted in rock gardens or as lawn substitutes. A dozen or so species and their selections, as well as some exciting introductions, are readily available. (The shrubby veronicas, which I won't have room to describe in this article, are sometimes classified in the genus *Hebe*.)

The easiest way to get started with veronicas is to purchase plants or to propagate existing plants by cuttings or division. Many veronicas are widely available in garden centers and nurseries, but the newly introduced species and cultivars are most readily found at specialty mail-order suppliers. (See Sources on p. 50.) You can also grow veronicas from seed, but the plants will vary somewhat.

Growing veronicas is simple. Most thrive in full sun or up to a half-day of shade, but a few, including *Veronica repens* and *V. filiformis*, do fine in dense shade. Few veronicas are fussy about soil; they'll grow equally well in clay, sandy loam or gravel. If a veronica doesn't grow well where you planted it, you can move it with impunity almost any time of year—just dig it up with a spadeful of soil, replant it and water it in thoroughly.

Photo, facing page: Chris Curless; illustration: Rosalind Loeb Wanke

In general, all veronicas do well in a wide range of moisture conditions—they don't rot during prolonged wet periods or suffer too much in a drought. However, the taller species do seem to like a bit more water. I've also noticed that veronicas with lighter green leaves, such as *V. fili-formis*, tend to grow better with more moisture, while those with darker green leaves, such as *V. pectinata* and *V. liwanensis*, tolerate longer periods of drought. Fertilizer and mulch aren't necessary, but applying them won't be detrimental.

Veronicas for perennial borders

With deep blue flowers the color of an alpine lake, germander speedwell (*V. latifolia*, formerly known as *V. teucrium*) is one of the most popular veronicas. It has a number of cultivars, although nowadays you are most apt to run across 'Crater Lake Blue', which, incidentally, looks much like nearly every other form of the species. A typical plant of germander speedwell forms a low mound 4 in. to nearly 1 ft. in height and three or four times as wide, growing larger with more soil fertility and moisture. In late spring, cascades of blue, star-shaped flowers completely obscure the mound of leaves. In hot weather, the display may last only a few weeks, but at higher elevations and in cooler climates, this veronica makes a vibrant pool of true blue color that lasts for over a month, beginning in late May.

Germander speedwell tolerates any loamy soil, from mildly acid to quite alkaline. I've sandwiched it between a native prickly pear and bear's breeches, in a spot where it is often scorched by the hot sun and usually neglected. Nonetheless, it still spreads dependably, though slowly, and blooms its heart out every spring. In most climates, it lives almost as long as peonies or epimediums, the ultimate garden Methuselahs.

Few garden perennials spread as inexorably or grow as well in a wider spectrum of soils and moisture levels as spike speedwell (*V. spicata*). The true species produces blue flowers, but some cultivars and those grown from seed produce flowers ranging from pure white and confectionary pink through blue and lavender. In flower, the most dwarf forms grow only 5 in. to 6 in. high, while the tallest ones reach heights of up to 18 in. The flowers last through much of late spring, and the plants bloom again if they're promptly deadheaded. All spike speedwells make neat mats of oval, scalloped, evergreen leaves. I can't imagine a garden without at least two or three forms of this stalwart perennial. It works well planted in the front of a border, at the edge of a woodland path or even as a small-scale ground cover.

The rosy-pink flowers of 'Red Fox', a 15-in. tall veronica, create a beautiful display in a perennial border or planted as a medium-height ground cover.

Photo: David Cavagnaro

Even the smallest garden has room for mat-forming veronicas. Blanketed by cobalt blue flowers, Turkish speedwell hugs the ground alongside a pink aster and white-flowered *Anacyclus depressus.*

Hoary speedwell (*V. incana*) looks like a spike veronica whose leaves have been dipped in flour. The flowers seem to be a purer, more sapphire blue than those of spike speedwell and are carried on taller stems. In most soils, hoary speedwell also spreads a trifle more slowly and grows better in warmer exposures than spike speedwell. Bloom time is in late spring to early summer.

V. longifolia, a Eurasian species, produces whorls of lance-shaped leaves on 4-ft. to 5-ft. tall stems, and is topped with feathery lavender, pale blue or white flowers in midsummer. *V. longifolia* is an invaluable addition to a prairie garden or the back of a border.

One of the veronicas frequently sold by nurseries, but one that I can live without, is gentian speedwell (*V. gentianoides*). The common name summons up images of a particularly luminous blue flower, but this veronica bears pallid blue flowers and resembles gentian only in its half-hearted mat of leaves. I find its cultivar, 'Variegata', which has white-edged leaves, far more interesting.

The silvery white leaves of hoary speedwell are a stunning sight year-round. In late spring and early summer, the fuzzy leaves provide a lovely foil for blue-purple flowers just beginning to open in the plant pictured here behind a rock ledge.

Veronicas for ground cover

The small, mat-forming veronicas are perfect for gardeners with limited space. As a rule of thumb, ground-cover veronicas do best with lots of sun. Otherwise, these prostrate plants are extremely unfussy about soil and site. They never need deadheading or much special attention other than watering during prolonged dry spells.

For many years, the only common groundcover veronica was *V. prostrata.* (This plant has been sold under a variety of names, including *V. allionii*, which is a smaller plant.) *V. prostrata* produces flat mats of deep evergreen leaves, up to an inch long, with neat serration around their edges. The leaves, arranged in a herringbone pattern along the stems, are completely hidden under a cloud of starry, blue flowers for almost a month in late spring. Spring is also the season of peak bloom for dianthus, penstemon and geraniums, with which speedwells combine beautifully. Various cultivars are available, but seed-grown plants are of equal merit, producing flowers that range in color from pure white,

Photos: top, Lauren Springer; right, Mark Kane

through various pink and lavender shades, and on into deep sapphire blue.

Few plants have greater durability, longevity or tolerance of abuse than *V. prostrata*. My oldest clumps at the Denver Botanic Gardens were planted in a heavy clay loam on a hot bank subject to periodic baking and frequent neglect. After ten years, these same plants are still producing displays equal to those of the first few years. I doubt if this species would persist very long without a little supplemental irrigation in our semi-arid climate, but in regions with slightly more rainfall, it should be indestructible.

Almost as well known as prostrate speedwell is combleaf speedwell (*V. pectinata*), grown for years mostly in its soft, gray-haired form, 'Rosea'. The watery pink flowers of this cultivar barely show up against its medium green leaves, but the species is gorgeous, with its dark green, inch-tall mat of leaves covered with sea-blue stars. Planted in a relatively fertile loam, it spreads even more quickly than 'Rosea', 5 in. to 8 in. each year, and grows thick enough to discourage weeds. In my gardens, the blue form reblooms quite well in late summer, and there is hardly a warm day all winter long when I don't find a few flowers peaking out between the wedge-shaped, furry leaves. It makes a wonderful underplanting for late, red tulips and combines almost as well with candytuft or basket-of-gold alyssum. I rate the blue combleaf speedwell as the most under-utilized small perennial in American gardens.

Turkish speedwell (*V. liwanensis*) has come to be viewed as an almost perfect ground cover here in Colorado. This recent introduction somewhat resembles a succulent creeping thyme. Its dark green leaves conform to the contours of the earth, covering the ground as snugly and thoroughly as a glove. The cobalt flowers start to open as early as late April some years and continue blooming into June. Turkish veronica tolerates the hottest exposures and looks as good on unwatered clay as it does on rich loam.

Creeping speedwell (*V. repens*) is one of those infuriating plants that looks irresistible in a pot in the nursery, but loses half its mystique once planted in the ground. Its steely blue-green, nearly oval leaves make a dense, cushiony mat when watered and fertilized regularly in a nursery, but degenerate into a rangy mat in the garden. A modest number of silvery

'Icicle', one of the few white-flowered veronicas, blooms all summer. This 18-in. tall cultivar makes a calming backdrop for hot-colored flowers.

SOURCES

These mail-order nurseries carry a wide selection of veronicas.

Carroll Gardens, 444 East Main St., P.O. Box 310, Westminster, MD 21157, 301-848-5422. Catalog $2, refundable with first order.

Joyce's Garden, 64640 Old Bend Redmond Highway, Bend, OR 97701, 503-388-4680. Catalog $2.

Rice Creek Gardens, Inc., 11506 Hwy. 65, Blaine, MN, 55434 612-754-8090 from 9 am to 5 pm. Catalog $2.

Siskyou Rare Plant Nursery, 2825 Cummings Road, Medford, OR 97501, 503-772-6846. Catalog $2, refundable with first order.

Surry Gardens, P.O. Box 145, Surry, ME 04684, 207-667-4493. Free list, catalog $2.

blue flowers are sprinkled over the plant in early spring. Creeping speedwell seems to demand particularly rich loam and more frequent irrigation and fussing than it deserves. It may perform better for others, but in my experience, this is one of the least useful veronicas.

Fastidious gardeners are sure to avoid the bird's-eye veronica (*V. filiformis*), which covers the ground with a prostrate film of apple-green, scalloped leaves the size of a pencil eraser. In early spring, this lovely veronica is liberally spangled with azure, two-tone flowers, but unfortunately, it covers the ground rampantly, becoming as irrepressible a lawn weed as violets. Yet if you like the latter, you'll also want to grow this undeniably beautiful veronica.

Veronicas for the rock garden

Many tiny veronicas from western Asia are trophies for rock gardeners, who are lovers of minutiae. These small plants do best in full sun and extremely well-drained soil composed mostly of gravel and sand, which will prevent fungal or bacterial infections on the plant's woolly leaves. The tufted speedwell (*V. caespitosa*) forms a mound an inch or so high that is covered with dense hairs and studded with bright blue flowers in early spring. Thymeleaf speedwell (*V. thymoides*) has leaves that are even more silvery and flowers that are bluer than those of tufted speedwell, and its flowers open a few weeks later in the season. Oriental speedwell (*V. orientalis*) forms a low mound of thyme-like leaves and clouds of midnight blue flowers in late spring. Ashen speedwell (*V. cinerea*) is very similar to the previous species, with even more silvery leaves and paler blue flowers. The gem of the western Asian veronicas, however, is the cottony speedwell (*V. bombycina*). This species of veronica has leaves of impossible whiteness that are attractive in their own right, but with its subtly contrasting, silvery blue flowers, cottony speedwell is irresistible.

I encourage you to try veronicas in your garden. I've been delighted to discover that with little effort, my gardens have become filled with more and more veronicas. I see no reason why yours can't, too. □

Panayoti Kelaidis gardens in Denver, Colorado, and is curator of the Rock Alpine Garden at Denver Botanic Gardens.

Photo: David Cavagnaro

Spring Beauties for the Shade

Native and exotic plants that thrive under a leafy canopy

Spring sunlight filters through the young leaves of burr oak and ash onto author Rodgers and her woodland garden. Bordering a suburban street, the garden is filled with spring-blooming plants.

by Aileen Detter Rodgers

Smack in the middle of the Great Plains, Nebraska might seem an unlikely place for a woodland garden. Yet for the past 30 years, I've grown hundreds of woodland plants under the shade of magnificent ash trees and burr oaks on my suburban property in Lincoln, the state's capital city. Over the years,

I've tried many woodland plants in the garden, native and exotic, wild and domesticated, and would like to share some of my favorites.

When I first saw the property, in April 1959, I knew I'd found a good home for my minuscule collection of wild woodland flowers that had become accustomed to sharing crowded quarters under a lilac bush. A double row of ash and burr oak trees, bounded on the street side by a lilac hedge, shaded a strip about 40 ft. deep along the

new property's 140-ft. frontage.

I dug several long, narrow beds, their free-form shapes pooling around the tree trunks, leaving a wide grassy path between the rows of trees. After digging large amounts of peat moss and compost into the beds, I set out my little collection— half a dozen to a dozen clumps each of Virginia bluebells, bloodroot, hepaticas, wild ginger, *Phlox divaricata,* Solomon's-plume and *Anemone canadensis.*

It was easy enough to

spade up a bed or two for special treasures, but the large site cried out for great swaths and swales of wildings, the sort of thing you see pictured on the cans of wildflower seed mixes sold today. Then, as fall approached, I began to have visions of daffodil drifts and other bulbs highlighting my wildings. So, instead of a strictly native woodland garden, I decided to aim for a shade garden with the appearance of naturalized growth. Short on time and money, I had to work on the dream slowly. Fortu-

Among the earliest plants to flower in Rodgers' garden are winter aconites, which brighten the brisk days of March.

nately, that meant the many errors I perpetrated were of small scale and easier to cope with.

Today, the ashes and oaks are much larger, and have proved excellent trees for underplanting (not all trees are). Beneath their high canopy, I've planted an understory of redbuds, dogwoods and yews. Half a dozen crab apples and Japanese maples set between the driveway and the property line have added another 30-ft. by 80-ft. area to the woodland and some lovely color to springtime. A great deal of sunlight penetrates the multilayered canopy in spring, rousing the woodland plants from dormancy and spurring most of them to bloom.

Bulbs

The first autumn, I planted three dozen bloom-size daffodil bulbs—including 'February Gold', 'Unsurpassable', 'Grapefruit' and 'Carlton'—that I'd dug from my previous garden. I knew that if I spaced them 8 in. apart they'd multiply and bloom undisturbed for many years. For early bloom, I ordered 100 snowdrops, 50 aconites and 24 scillas, all native to damp woodlands in the lower elevations of southwestern European mountain ranges. Aconites (*Eranthis hyemalis*) are less well known than snowdrops, perhaps because they're harder to establish. The flowers (shown in the top photo), 1½-in.-wide golden buttercups set atop a green

topknot of fringy leaves, are very bright and cheery in the chill of March. *Scilla Tubergeniana*, a 3-in. raceme of tightly packed watery-blue flowers, seemed perfect for a narrow dry stream of flowers meandering and widening through bare woody trunks in the spring.

It's uncharacteristic of me to order large quantities of any one plant, but previously I'd had little luck with snowdrops and aconites, and wanted to try several sites, planting dozens in each, hoping to hit upon a successful take. Whether it was the site or planting the bulbs in larger numbers of their own kind, or both, several plantings took off in abundance.

To be enjoyed at close range, I knew that these small earliest-of-early flowers needed to border the paths. There they'd also receive sunlight from February to May, summer shade and no competition from other plants. But planting bulbs on the edges of grass paths would be problematic—the mower would cut immature bulb foliage along with the grass. So I turned under the grass, at the same time reshaping the paths to meander more. I planted the bulbs in the new bays and pockets and topped the paths with pine needles. The snowdrops and aconites have self-seeded and produced more bulbs generously, but the scillas

never have. Once established, all three bulbs can be moved with ease; this is best done when they're in full bloom, by digging a small sod (a cluster of bulbs surrounded by earth).

Naturalized perennials

Deciding to include nonnative plants opened a floodgate of possibilities. Between gardenclub sale tables and gardening neighbors, I could garner great quantities of plants. Four of my early acquisitions have been especially important in the garden: forget-me-nots, pink campion, Lenten roses and spring-beauties. They're my workhorses, my thoroughbreds, my beauties.

Perennial forget-me-nots (*Brunnera macrophylla*) bloom in early April here, beginning with a delicate fretwork of stems holding trueblue forget-me-not flowers above a small mound of heart-shaped leaves. As the season unfolds, flower stems increase in quantity and grow to 24 in. This goes on for six weeks of jeweled blue bloom. As the flowers fade, the stems set seed and drop back somewhat to be hidden among the leaves, which increase in width to 8 in. The green mound of leaves is very attractive and somewhat drought-resistant for the rest of the summer. Brunnera does seed around, especially in wet years, but it took me 20 years to have enough plants. Now I cull the plantings after bloom

Small but tough, spring-beauties colonized the garden's paths, and bloom for about a month in late April and early May.

Peals of Virginia bluebells hang from 2-ft.-tall stalks in late April.

and pull out the seedlings.

Pink campion (*Silene dioica*) is dioecious—having both male and female plants—and biennial. The female plants seed about copiously and the seedlings can be thinned or not as you wish. First-year plants are small, soft light-green leaf mounds. In late April of the second spring, they send aloft sturdy, branched stems, 18 in. long, sprinkled with 1-in.-wide, clear-rose flowers. Each flower has rounded petals and a long green calyx, the female plants showing puffy fat calyxes. Six weeks of showy bloom follow.

Lenten roses (*Helleborus orientalis*) are long-lived perennials. My original clump is 25 years old. The flower buds are present and protected by old, usually dead leaves as early as January. The buds swell in March and, if snow is gone and spring early, they rise in the same month on stems 10 in. to 12 in. long, three or four to a stem. Hellebore blooms are not damaged by frost unless temperatures drop well below 20°F, but they seem to time their flowering with uncanny accuracy, and are rarely frozen. The blooms are shaped somewhat like single roses, 2 in. across. They range in color from white to wine-stippled ivory to solid-chocolate wine. The new foliage unfolds after bloom into palmate, leathery, dark-green leaves, as attractive as the flowers are. I've cut the foliage for indoor arrangements, but that's a mistake because it greatly weakens the plant. Hellebores are evergreen in climates milder than mine. My plants began producing a few seedlings after four or five years and do so readily now, but are in no way a nuisance. Seedlings pull up easily and are in demand by friends.

My first spring-beauties (*Claytonia virginica*, shown at center on the facing page) appeared so slight and frail, even pale, when I received them that I wasn't sure they'd grow. They're small plants (arising from tiny bulbs), so I put them along the path edge and hoped for the best. The

Woodland plants contribute more than flowers to the spring garden. Above, large bloodroot leaves and the smaller three-lobed leaves of hepatica frame a bouquet of tiny rue anemone (*Anemonella thalictroides*) flowers. Below, daisylike bloodroot flowers sparkle in the garden for a week or so in early spring. The leaves follow, reaching 5 in. across, and make a handsome ground cover the rest of the growing season.

next spring, an unprepossessing, languid growth of pale ½-in. flowers appeared, each flower with rose veins and thin 2-in. straps of succulent leaves. Not very exciting. From then on I forgot them. Three or four years later, I began to notice nice patches of palest pink out in the paths as well as along the edges. Well, I thought, those will soon be trampled out. But very few succumbed. They loved the paths and wormed a place into my heart in a big way. Today they ramp and thrive in the most unexpected places, though never intruding selfishly. Weeding the paths is such a pleasure during spring-beauty time, about a month in late April and early May.

Wildflowers

Of the wildflowers I brought with me from my previous garden, I recommend four highly. Virginia bluebells (*Mertensia virginica*) is an easy perennial. It grows from thick, brittle rootstocks, the soft light-green leaf shoots emerging quickly in early April. The hanging bluebell flowers, which follow in late April, harbor a hint of pink. After seeding in late May, the plant dies down and goes dormant. Plants are easy to transplant at any time, even if you don't get all the roots. This species self-seeds readily, and once you have enough plants, severe curbing is in order. Before the seeds develop enough to ripen, I yank all the spent bloom heads and drop them where they're pulled so as not to take more from the soil than goes in. The remains dry up quickly and are hidden in my garden by wild ageratum (*Eupatorium coelestinum*), a late-August-blooming plant that shows shoots in June.

In late March, the silver-gray leaves of bloodroot (*Sanguinaria canadensis*) appear, each third-year leaf clasping a thick white bud. These patiently wait until the first warm, sunny day, then bingo, white daisy stars wink open throughout the whole shade garden (see the photo at left). If it's quite windy, the petals blow away quickly; otherwise the show lasts a week or two. There is a lovely sterile double-flowered form (the cultivar 'Multiplex'), expensive, but worth it. After bloom the leaves develop, one round gray-green pedestal to a plant. Bloodroot has self-seeded happily in my garden from the beginning, and I have moved clumps in bloom. There are never too many.

Phlox divaricata, a Nebraska native, is ubiquitous on our property. In April and May, narrow-leaved 12-in. stems support heads of lavender-blue flowers, ¾ in. across, opening through a period of six weeks. Blue phlox, or sweet William as it's fondly called here, lives a few years and spreads by seed. To control *P. divaricata*, I pull on the whole plant before seeds ripen. Those that pull up roots and all are the culls; the rest, losing just their seed stems, are about the right number of plants for another year. I've tried special color variants, such as white, eyed or deeper blue, but these have always gradually melded back into the type, as the seedlings don't come true.

My *Hepatica americana* is an early bird. In March, I pull back fallen oak leaves and locate the plants by the previous year's dead leaves. Underneath are clusters of furry pink buds like tiny newborn bunnies in a nest. The flowers aren't showy, but are utterly charming. They open above the leaves in a week or so, depending on the weather, becoming 3-in.-high nosegays of apple-blossom-like bloom lasting for two weeks or more if the weather is cool. *H. americana* and its similar relative *H. acutiloba* both grow for me, but in different places. *H. americana* seems to prefer more acid soil and more pine duff. Flowers of both are white, blue or pink, and both have tripartite foliage. Darker leaves usually indicate darker flower colors, though I'm convinced that color depends on location—I've moved special colors only to have them pale in their new spot.

Ground covers

To cover the great expanse of shade garden, I sought out

ground-cover plants. At first, my wild ginger (*Asarum canadense*) seemed the perfect plant. A hardy deciduous perennial, it spreads to form a uniform neat green carpet, low and compact. But after ten years of mutual respect, this plant suddenly became hysterical. In late summer, small seedlings appeared everywhere except sunny, dry places. If I didn't catch them then, it took a tool to pry them out later when they'd developed runners. Between mature plants and seedlings, the plant threatened to overwhelm all neighboring plants. I'm still at war.

Other ground covers have proved less problematic. The tallest, presenting 12-in.-high, flat umbrellas of green, is mayapple (*Podophyllum peltatum*, shown at left). In some areas it tends to romp lustily, so it needs watching, but mayapple generally stays where it's planted. Creeping forget-me-not (*Omphalodes verna*) is a slowly spreading plant 5 in. high with blue flowers in April. It's not a heavy bloomer. Sweet woodruff (*Galium odoratum*) is a delicate-appearing colonizer. Its white flowers are fleeting, and its foliage is sweet-smelling when bruised. Epimediums are the queens of ground covers. They're rather expensive and slow, but worth the wait. All they need are shade, water and medium-rich soil. They bloom before leaves appear, in April—nice spots of red, pink, yellow or white on a tangle of 12-in. stems. They're drought-tolerant in summer. *Mahonia repens* spreads by short runners to make a thin cover of evergreen hollylike foliage on 3-in. woody stems. It's easy to grow and interesting in texture, and occasionally it bears lovely gold flower clusters in May. Of all these ground covers, only sweet woodruff wants extra water during our dry summers.

Here today...

Of course, not every plant I've tried in the woods has succeeded. Primroses are my biggest disappointment, though I haven't given up after all these years of their rejection.

Mayapple, with its large, deeply lobed leaves, makes an ideal ground cover. Mixed with lungwort (*Pulmonaria saccharata*, the shorter plants with spotted leaves above), mayapple rounds off an intersection in Rodgers' garden. In April, a lovely flower nestles under each leafy mayapple canopy (below).

They leave the garden at any time—winter, spring or summer. I don't know why they die. I've tried many locations and care routines, and the worst losses come after a few years of success when I try to divide a crowded clump. I like primroses so much that I replace them practically every year. Fortunately, plants in full bloom are now on the market at a low price.

Early on, I planned to have great expanses of ferns. It didn't work out that way. The only fern that grew in great abundance for me was ostrich fern (*Matteuccia Struthiopteris*). But it was so exuberant that I finally had to rogue it out completely. Many representatives of the fern family grow in Nebraska, but only three species are common in the woodlands nearby. These three—maidenhair fern (*Adiantum pedatum*), fragile fern (*Cystopteris fragilis*) and rattlesnake fern (*Botrychium virginianum*)—find a congenial habitat in the shade garden. They are small colonizers in the wild and remain so for me. I suppose the lesson here is the one learned by Dorothy in Oz: what you want is likely to be in your own backyard.

Success and failure are relative terms. A sort of natural succession seems to take place in my garden. Some plants are very permanent, such as the native ferns, hellebores, bloodroot and hepaticas. Most are semipermanent. A few thrive for ten to 15 years, then find growing difficult. The native columbines (*Aquilegia canadensis* var. *latiuscula*) that I grow are particularly unhappy now. Individual plants never lived long, but the seedlings regularly grew into magnificent plants. Now they're few and not as sturdy. Jack-in-the-pulpits (*Arisaema triphyllum*) have an opposite history. For years I had very few. Now there are many seedlings and the mature pulpits are huge, probing up 3 ft. sometimes.

Some plants don't take off until certain soil bacteria, fungi or pollinators are abundant enough. Wild ginger, for example, is pollinated by a specific beetle that visits the plant's ground-hugging floral

The complicated blossoms of native columbines (detail below) combine nicely with the simple white blooms of lungwort (above).

SOURCES

Between them, these sources offer all the plants mentioned in the text:

Busse Gardens, Rt. 2, Box 238, Cokato, MN 55321. Catalog $2.00.

Carroll Gardens, 444 E. Main St., P.O. Box 310, Westminster, MD 21157. Catalog $2.00.

McClure & Zimmerman, 108 W. Winnebago St., P.O. Box 368, Friesland, WI 53935. Catalog free.

Siskiyou Rare Plant Nursery, 2825 Cummings Rd., Medford, OR 97201. Catalog $2.00.

We-Du Nurseries, Rt. 5, Box 724, Marion, NC 28752. Catalog $1.00.

pouches. It took a while for the beetles to find my ginger. Now the plant is a menace in my garden.

Maintenance

A naturalized shade garden isn't the easy-care garden it might appear, even when fully planted. That which looks natural is not all that natural. Thus, I try to keep the upper hand, guiding, culling, roguing and transplanting. A big job is keeping ahead of greedy spreading plants. In addition to wild ginger, I've totally rejected Solomon's-plume, *Anemone canadensis*, *Scilla siberica* (this is so beautiful that I almost waited too long), various garden varieties of lamium, *Allium tricoccum* and *Anemone ranunculoides*. In addition, every year there are unwanted tree seedlings that need to be pulled.

Over the years, I've built up a surface of pine litter on the beds, and continually tossed on twigs and tree branches (broken into smaller pieces) that had fallen on the lawn. (I get a certain emotional release by gathering a few sticks that are messing up the lawn and flinging them right into the flower beds.) Other than initial preparation, this litter and each year's leaf drop are the only enrichment the garden beds have received. In the early years, I raked about half the year's leaf fall off the beds in the spring. Now I just clean up the paths and the plants alongside them, and completely clean off a large bed of aconites. The other plants seem to rise through the thick leaf covering very well.

Even a 30-year-old garden is never complete. Hostas are my newest additions. I'm spreading a collection of varieties over a large area that grew too shady for lawn grasses a few years ago. Between clumps, I've planted snowdrops and daffodils. The hostas make a nice transition to the lawn as well as between the seasons—they bloom in summer, when the blooms of my spring beauties are a memory. ☐

Aileen Detter Rodgers wrote about amaryllis in FG #5.

Hostas

A wealth of foliage for shady sites

The hosta 'Gold Standard', shown above, forms a mound of creamy-gold leaves edged in green. In 1988, the American Hosta Society selected this as the favorite hosta cultivar.

by Sam and Carleen Jones

We got bitten by the hosta bug eight years ago, and the more we've learned about these versatile, durable perennials, the more we like them. When we bought the property that is now Piccadilly Farm, we didn't know much about growing hostas, but we hoped they'd do well in the shade of the big old pines and hardwood trees that cover much of our land. They've done so well that they're now the specialty of the nursery business we started to keep us active during our retirement.

Hostas form clumps of foliage in a variety of colors, textures, sizes and shapes. The leaves may be green, gold or blue, or variegated with yellow or white. Often they have a waxy texture or lustrous sheen. Hosta leaves may be smooth, ribbed, corrugated or puckered. They range in shape from slender to rounded to heart-shaped, and they vary in size from smaller than a postage stamp to larger than a dinner plate. Hostas aren't evergreen—

they go dormant in the winter—but their leaves first show up in our garden in mid- to late March, and often the foliage is still attractive at Thanksgiving. And in addition, many cultivars have blue, violet or white blooms that look refreshingly cool in the heat of summer and early autumn.

There are about 25 species of hostas, mostly native to Japan, Korea and China, and hundreds of named cultivars. We have around 200 species and cultivars, but we're more interested in making a beautiful garden with hostas than in amassing a collection for its own sake. We enjoy designing with hostas, and trying new ways of combining them with each other and with other kinds of plants. They're the perfect plants for our kind of informal woodland gardening.

Using hostas in the garden

When we bought this land, a tangle of privet, poison ivy, blackberries and Japa-

nese honeysuckle grew under the pines, oaks, sweet gums, tulip poplars and dogwood trees, and there were steep hillsides and deep gullies to deal with. Fortunately, our oldest daughter is a landscape architect, and she helped us considerably by preparing a master site plan that located the roads, buildings, nursery area and display garden. Having the master plan guided our efforts as we worked to clear away the brush, thin and prune the trees, and make paths and terraces.

We started the garden on a small scale, using crossties to make three terraces on the steep east-facing slope that dropped from our newly built house to the creek and nursery area below. The soil was pure Georgia red clay, but we added five heaping pickup loads of well-rotted wood chips to the 30-ft. by 15-ft. area, and applied lime, superphosphate and 10-10-10 fertilizer. With much tilling and digging, we readied the area for planting, and set out our first hostas. Since then we've expanded the garden each year. Now it covers nearly two acres, and demonstrates many ways to use hostas.

Ground covers—We've tried several types and sizes of hostas as ground covers.

Masses of the larger inexpensive cultivars grow quickly to fill a space and shade out weeds, and their spreading roots and rhizomes can reduce soil erosion on steep banks. White-edged *Hosta undulata* 'Albo-marginata' and gold-leaved *H.* 'August Moon' (see photos, p. 59) are particularly nice for lighting up a dark area. Solid-green *H. lancifolia* provides an attractive foil for other plants and looks cool in the garden—that's especially welcome during our hot Georgia summers.

Drifts—One way we've created a natural effect is by planting hostas in drifts. Drifts are similar to a ground cover except that the plants are spaced as they might occur in nature: closer together in the center of the drift, then gradually thinning out along the margins to blend into other plantings. Using several dozen of the same kind of plant to make a drift gives a natural look. By contrast, a collection of one of this and one of that kind of plant usually has a dotted appearance. Drifts look especially good trailing down a slope, but even if you don't have a setting that looks natural, you can create your own. We used to live in town and had a rectangular subdivision lot, but we made it look more appealing by putting in curved beds and making drifts of plants.

Edgings—Hostas edge several of the garden paths, guiding visitors and distinguishing the beds. Tracing gentle curves, rather than straight lines, the hosta edging draws your eye along the path and invites you into the garden. Using too many of the same hostas as edging would be monotonous; instead, we've put in a variety and staggered them with other plants. Small gold hostas make interesting edgers; among our favorites is 'Gold Drop'. Visiting another garden, we saw *H. ventricosa* grown along the top of a rock wall, with the leaves drooping over the edge and softening the masonry construction. This gave us the idea of using hostas along the edge of a masonry pool in our garden. Similarly, we've used the large white-flowered *H. plantaginea* as a foundation planting around the base of our house.

Accents—Hostas with colored or variegated foliage serve well as accent plants— they call your attention by their placement, and by complementing or contrasting with surrounding plants. For example, we wanted something special at a junction of two paths. On one corner, we planted a hosta 'Frances Williams', which has large leaves with blue-green centers and gold edges, and flanked it with a choice epimedium and a golden-colored sedge that matches the gold of the hosta leaves. On the opposite corner, we used the gold hosta 'Piedmont Gold', and underplanted it with variegated pachysandra. Thus the color gold is repeated, to catch your eye and to tie it all together.

The Joneses grow hostas on the wooded hillsides of their Georgia property. They removed some trees and pruned others to supply the dappled shade that hostas prefer.

Hosta beds—We've gained a lot of satisfaction from designing garden beds that complement the rocky wooded slopes of our site. Most of our beds have irregular shapes and sizes, because we find them more interesting than geometric or uniform beds. Planting the area inside a bed can be as intriguing as piecing a quilt— we think about leaf colors, textures and sizes; clump shape and size; and overall effect.

Carleen does most of the designing, using what we jokingly call the "pot method." When we're ready to plant a new garden area or rework an old one, she looks at the space from all angles. Once she has a mental picture of the scene she's attempting to develop, we discuss the plans and work out our differences of opinion. Rather than make a design on paper, we bring plants in pots from the nursery, place them on the beds, and shift them around to observe the effects of different kinds of plants and spacings. If you're buying plants, you can use the pot method to fine-tune a design before you dig the holes to set them in place.

We've filled some beds primarily with hostas. For example, in one triangular bed, we used 'Blue Angel', a large blue-leaved hosta, as the focal point. It's flanked by the sheen of white-margined 'Fringe Benefit', the luster of light-gold 'Gold Standard', and the bright-gold color and thick texture of 'Zounds' and 'Midas Touch'. 'Resonance' provides a complementary ground cover to the front. The ends of the bed taper out with the nice blues of 'Blue Boy', 'Blue Wedgwood' and *H. tokudama*, and the golds of 'Gold Drop' and 'Golden Prayers'. One way we created variety in this bed was by using different numbers of the different plants. Some of our customers want to buy everything in groups of three, but we like to use plants singly, in pairs, in threes, and in larger numbers.

Spacing—It's taken us time to learn how to space hostas in the garden. As beginners, we didn't know about the growth rates, clump sizes or foliage characteristics of mature hostas—it's something you can't predict by looking at plants in a nursery, and have to observe over time in the garden. When a clump of hostas grows in the same place for several years, undisturbed, both the leaves and the overall clump change in appearance. For example, a new division of *H. sieboldiana* 'Ele-

Growing for a few years in the same place, these hostas have reached their mature size and form. *H. sieboldiana* 'Elegans' (rear left) has cupped blue-green leaves 12 in. in diameter. *H.* 'Ginko Craig' (front left), *H.* 'Gold Drop' (front center) and *H. ventricosa* 'Aureo-marginata' form smaller leaves and clumps.

Rather than design on paper, Carleen Jones tries out different arrangements and combinations of plants by moving the pots around on the prepared bed before planting.

gans' in a 1-gal. can usually has leaves 4 in. to 5 in. in diameter. A mature plant of the same cultivar has leaves 12 in. to 14 in. in diameter; one specimen that's been in our garden for five years has made a clump 6 ft. across. The year after we planted our first hostas, some clumps were already touching each other, while others had a lot of ground showing around them. Now we know to plant small-growing hostas on 12-in. centers, medium hostas on 20-in. centers and large ones on 36-in. centers. In masses of a single cultivar, we set the plants a bit closer together so their leaves will interweave.

With other plants—Often we combine hostas with other shade-loving plants, to fill the spaces between clumps in a new bed, or to provide contrast in color, texture and height. Impatiens are good for filling the gaps between hostas, and they flower through a long part of the season. We usually choose white or deep-red impatiens. They self-sow here and repeat for a few years until the hostas fill in and shade out the seedlings.

Hostas are vigorous plants and will come up readily through perennial ground covers such as sweet woodruff, ajuga, mondo grass and wild sweet William (*Phlox divaricata*). Other perennials that make good companions for hostas are daffodils, which bloom before the hostas emerge; hardy ferns, whose delicate fronds contrast well with hostas' more substantial leaves; and lacy-leaved flowering perennials such as astilbe, columbine and wild bleeding-heart (*Dicentra exima*).

Like any gardeners, sometimes we make mistakes in placing our plants—we set them too close, for example, or try combinations that just don't work out right. Learning from your mistakes is part of gardening, and we aren't reluctant to simply dig things up and move them around later. Hostas can be moved at any season with no ill effect other than a minor setback in size the following season.

Buying and growing hostas

Hostas are sold in containers or as bare-root plants at garden centers around the country and by specialty mail-order nurseries (see Resources, p. 60). The price for a single plant can be as little as $2 or as much as $200 or more, depending on how rare the cultivar is, with plenty of choices in the $5 to $20 range.

Container-grown plants suffer little if any shock from transplanting, because the roots remain intact. Bare-root plants are fine if they've been properly stored. Look for large divisions that haven't dried out, and that seem to be sound and free of rot. Soak their roots in water for an

hour or two, then plant them promptly. When putting hostas into the ground, be sure that the crown—the place where roots and shoots emerge—is just barely below the surface of the soil. Planting a hosta too deeply stunts its growth.

Selecting a site—Hostas are such tough, durable plants that they'll survive poor siting, mistreatment and neglect. But to help them look their best, site selection is very important. Hostas grow best on a site with some shade from the sun, especially in the South, but how much shade is enough? It's difficult to say, because there are so many kinds of shade—the shade of a house, a hedge or fence, a conifer, or a deciduous tree are all different. The shade under our pine trees is a hot shade—a lot of sun comes through. The hardwood trees make a cool shade in the summer, but offer scant protection to early-sprouting hostas that emerge before the trees leaf out in the spring.

Within limits, the more sun a clump gets, the more shoots it will form, and the better it will look. The leaves may be smaller and shorter, but they'll have a thicker texture and better color, and the clump will be denser and more compact. The trick is to give hostas as much sun as possible without scalding the foliage. Sun-damaged leaves turn sort of a creamy color, and their texture changes—normally thick ones get thin, as if you'd scraped off the surface with a razor blade.

Sun tolerance varies considerably among cultivars. Those with white-centered leaves are most vulnerable to sun and drought here in the South. The white part of a leaf has no chlorophyll, and it is weaker than the green part and can literally shred and collapse in the heat of summer. Cultivars derived from *H. plantaginea* have the most sun tolerance. We experiment, make observations, and move plants around if we need to, following the general rule that hostas tolerate morning sun better than afternoon sun. Avoid dry sites that drain too quickly and don't retain water. Hostas are much more prone to sunburn if the soil is dry.

Preparing the soil—Proper soil preparation is a key to success with hostas. We've done a lot to improve our rocky, red Georgia clay. Where we can get in with a tractor, we use a subsoil cultivator to break up the hardpan, and a tiller attachment to work the soil to a depth of 8 in. or so. To add organic matter to the soil, we usually use compost or ground pine bark, which are relatively stable and take a few years to decompose. Early on, we made the mistake of using masses of freshly raked leaves in a bed, but when they decomposed over the winter the bed settled, the hostas sank, and we had to lift and replant them.

When we're working around tree roots, instead of a tractor we use a mattock to

Hostas to start with

H. undulata **'Albo-marginata'** forms a medium-size clump of green leaves bordered with cream, and has lavender flowers in June.

H. **'Blue Angel'** makes a very large tiered mound of heavily textured blue leaves that can be as wide as 18 in. in diameter.

H. **'Ginko Craig'** forms low, horizontal mounds of dark-green leaves with neat white margins. It has deep-blue flowers in summer.

H. **'August Moon'** forms a large clump of crinkled, heavily textured leaves that stay gold-colored all season. It has white flowers.

H. lancifolia is a fast-growing hosta that forms a cascading mound of green strap-shaped leaves, and has lavender flowers in September.

H. venusta makes a dwarf, spreading clump of tiny, heart-shaped green leaves, and has light-purple flowers. It's ideal for rock gardens.

loosen the soil and get the rocks out. Then we add enough soil and ground bark to raise the beds a few inches and make them easier to plant. The tree roots quickly grow up into the soil that we've improved, but our hostas don't seem to suffer from the competition. We do know one collector who grows his plants in pots sunk into the ground, to keep the hosta roots separate from the nearby tree roots.

We fertilize our hostas by broadcasting a light application of granular 10-10-10 in the early spring, just when the leaves appear. Sometimes we follow this with a light dose of ammonium nitrate in the summer. Hostas don't need heavy fertilizing, particularly if they're growing in well-prepared soil. We use an overhead sprinkler system to water the beds throughout the season, whenever the weather is dry. Other than that, the hostas in our display garden require little maintenance.

Potted hostas—Hostas grow in pots as well as in the ground. Even the largest cultivars can be kept in 3-gal. containers for years. We know gardeners who grow hostas in urns and planters on their patios; one displays a potted *H. sieboldiana* 'Elegans' on her fireplace hearth all summer (setting it in a cool place outdoors for the necessary winter dormancy). In our nursery, we grow most of the hostas in square plastic 1-gal. containers, and put some in 3-gal. cans to produce large specimens. We make a potting mix from 6 parts ground pine bark, 1 part coarse sand, and 1 part woods soil, amended with superphosphate, dolomitic limestone and 10-10-10 fertilizer. Each spring we fertilize the plants in containers with additional 10-10-10 and Osmocote 14-14-14 (a timed-release fertilizer). In the North, hostas in pots must be protected from extremely cold weather, either by being sunk into the ground, stored in a cold frame, or surrounded with a mulch or cover for insulation.

Pests and diseases

Our warm, humid Georgia climate favors snails and slugs that feed on hostas. We watch for holes in the leaves, and spread methaldehyde bait to control these pests, usually applying it twice during the growing season. Keeping the garden tidy and removing leaf litter also help to reduce the populations of these pests.

Several years ago, we noticed that some of our hostas were disappearing into the ground. When we pulled them up, we were surprised to see that the roots had been neatly chewed away. The Extension Wildlife Biologist at the University of Georgia explained that the culprit was a small rodent known as the pine vole. We've tried dropping pellets of rat poison down into the vole tunnels or placing the pellets under buckets (to protect our pets and keep the pellets dry), but adding more cats to our family has also

helped control these varmints. If spotted in time, damaged plants can be potted and nurtured back to good health.

Deer can seriously damage hostas. Our two dogs keep the deer away from the garden area adjacent to our home, and we clip the dogs and spread their hair in an area of the nursery where deer have been browsing. So far it's served as an effective repellent.

We've had to deal with two other problems in the recent hot, dry summers. Black blister beetles, which chew the edges of hosta leaves, especially those with a white margin, are easily controlled with a carbaryl insecticide such as Sevin. Southern blight is a fungal disease that attacks peanuts, tomatoes and several other crops. On hostas, the fungus weakens the petiole of a leaf at ground level, causing the leaf to fall over. When we see an infected plant, we remove the damaged leaves and drench the clump as well as the surrounding area with the fungicide PCNB, sold under the trade name Terrachlor.

Division and propagation

Unlike so many other perennials, hostas in a garden do not require frequent division—a clump can grow in the same place for 20 years or more. If a plant is doing well, we don't disturb it. Hostas aren't aggressive and don't crowd out other plants. Moreover, we choose not to divide the hostas in our display garden

because we want to see them reach their maximum potential size.

Division, however, is the best way to propagate hostas. You can divide them throughout the growing season, but in our nursery, we usually do it in July and August, allowing the plants to reestablish before fall frost. After digging up a plant and shaking the soil off its roots, we examine the rhizomes. Rhizomes are horizontal underground stems, long and slender in some hostas but thick and compact in others. A tangle of thick fleshy roots radiates down from the rhizomes. New leaves and flower stalks grow up from distinct buds. Often we can divide clumps by just pulling the rhizomes apart; other clumps require cutting with a sharp knife. Either way, the important thing is that each division have at least one good-size bud. The larger the division the better, as small divisions develop very slowly.

If you want to propagate from a large, established clump, use a sharp spade to cut a pie-shaped wedge out of the clump in the very early spring, just as new growth is emerging. Refill the hole with some good compost. Then you can further divide the wedge, or plant it as is to start a new clump. In replanting, be sure to keep the crown at the same level as before—add or remove soil from the bottom of the hole until you've got it right.

H. ventricosa is the only hosta that we regularly propagate by seed. It has an unusual type of reproduction in which the embryo develops directly from maternal tissue, so the seedlings are exactly identical to the mother plant. Many other hostas produce seeds abundantly, but we don't normally sow them. The seedlings of hybrid cultivars don't come true to type, and are almost always disappointing compared to their parents. When we do raise a batch of seedlings from time to time, we cull them severely to eliminate the majority that are plain and ordinary, and save only the few plants that show interesting leaf form, color and texture.

The modern way to propagate hostas is through tissue culture, a specialized technique that requires a sterile laboratory. We don't do it ourselves, but many of the hostas we buy have been propagated that way. Tissue culture has a few drawbacks. Not all plants come true to type, and even when carefully screened, not all offspring make the grade. Further, some cultivars don't grow well when produced by tissue culture. But the advantage of tissue culture is that it brings new cultivars to the marketplace at affordable prices—plants that would have sold for $300 a few years ago can be purchased for $20 to $25 now. □

Sam Jones is professor of botany at the University of Georgia. Carleen Jones is a retired biology teacher. Their garden and nursery is near Bishop, Georgia.

Last year's shoot

This year's shoot

How hostas grow

Hosta leaves grow out of a short, compact stem called a rhizome. At the base of each leaf is a bud; one or more of these buds develop and produce the following year's shoots. A clump can be divided by pulling or cutting apart the rhizome between the shoots.

Bud

(Roots have been cut away to expose rhizome.)

Roots

Rhizome

Planting hostas—A newly purchased hosta may have a single shoot (right). Be sure to position the plant so that the crown—the point where the shoot grows out of the rhizome (indicated by Carleen's index finger)—is just barely covered with soil. After growing in the same spot for several years, a single plant will have multiplied to produce dozens of shoots (far right).

Illustration: Laura B. Goodwin; photo, left: Staff

The showy flowers of penstemons, such as those of 'Firebird' (above), are a vibrant addition to any landscape. They bloom in late spring to midsummer. With a large selection to choose from, most gardeners can find one well-suited to their conditions.

Penstemons for the Garden

Red, white and true blue perennials

by Gwen Kelaidis

Penstemons have unlimited potential as garden plants, but are often dismissed as mere natives, too wild to tame into cultivated flowers. Related to snapdragons, penstemons bear similar spires of open, tubular, showy flowers in blue, purple, white, scarlet, pink and occasionally even yellow. Depending on the species, they bloom from late April through August.

These herbaceous perennials range from 6 ft. to less than an inch tall and from stout to slender. The shrubby species remain evergreen, but in cold climates, most other penstemons die back to their basal foliage in winter. Penstemons last an average of only five years in cultivation, but they're easy to renew from seeds or cuttings.

All penstemons are native to North and Central America, south to Guatemala. Most are from the Southwest and the Great Basin (Utah, Nevada and Idaho), but they can be found, and cultivated, in all of the U.S. They hail from diverse habitats, including the highest mountains, tallgrass prairies, sandy creek washes, deserts, oil shale barrens and woodlands.

In the garden

I've grown over 100 penstemon species, and there are still over 150 more left for me to try. (My fellow penstemon lovers and I refer to ourselves as pentstemaniacs.) In part, I grow penstemons to remind me of all their native habitats and the beauty of our country. They also have led me into many an adventure, searching for the best species for my gardens.

A hackneyed criticism of penstemons, and one that I sometimes levy myself, is that they have little substance when not in flower. Penstemons are not bushy plants. In most species, the majority of leaves are at ground level, splayed out in a loose rosette.

Penstemons

- Herbaceous perennials
- 1 in. to 6 ft. tall, depending on species or cultivar
- Bloom spring to midsummer; flower colors include blue, purple, white, scarlet, pink and yellow
- Most prefer full sun
- Require good drainage
- Many do best in dry soils; some tolerate moist soils.
- Easy to propagate
- Hardy in USDA Zones 1 to 10, depending on species or cultivar
- Use in borders, xeriscapes, rock gardens

The foxglove penstemon, a 1½-ft.-tall native of moist prairies and grasslands, is adapted to a wide range of climatic conditions.

In flower, penstemons fill vertical and horizontal space in the garden, but once the stems are cut back after bloom, the plants lack presence. This is of little consequence in a rock garden or a xeriscape, where a sparser look is part of the design, but it's problematic in a traditional perennial border.

You can't fill the gaps by spacing penstemons close to neighboring plants, since they don't do well when crowded. But you could pair them with plants such as baby's-breath that won't smother the penstemons. Depending upon your border design, you could also place 14-in.- to 18-in.-tall penstemons just behind prostrate edging plants, so the pruned-back penstemons look like part of the low edge.

Penstemons are quite new on the gardening scene—even the best known have been cultivated for fewer than 50 years. Hybridizers at the University of Nebraska in North Platte have developed penstemons that are better adapted to garden conditions, selecting them for a compact habit, a broad range of colors and longevity.

Not all penstemons have similar cultural requirements. Learning to grow each species well is a challenge and a wonderful opportunity to learn about how plants adapt to garden conditions. If you get really involved with penstemons, you'll want to learn more about the different taxonomic groups, or sections, of this genus. In some cases, species within a section have similar cultural requirements, which can help you figure out how to grow uncommon ones. To learn more about penstemons, join The American Penstemon Society (see Resources on p. 67).

Nearly all penstemons require good drainage, and most need a sunny site. Beyond that, their native habitats offer clues to successfully growing and using them in the garden. Penstemons have a pioneer spirit. Though found in all kinds of habitats, they seem to thrive in the poorest conditions. The western species, in particular, are plants of gravel slides, road cuts and barren hills—all dry, well-drained sites. They thrive

Photos: facing page, Thomas E. Eltzroth; above, Pamela Harper in open places, without much competition from other plants. This makes them suitable for rock gardens, xeriscapes and dryland borders.

The more midwestern and eastern species tend to be native to grasslands. All of them are more successful in a traditional, irrigated perennial border than their dryland relatives. The shrubby species from the Northwest, which are often from the high mountains, also tolerate more moisture, but demand sharp drainage and winter shade as well. The gardener who aspires to grow all of the penstemons must have a varied garden indeed! Yet almost any gardener in the United States can grow a few species of these beautiful flowers.

To help you get started, I'll introduce you to some penstemons that are suited for different climate conditions and garden uses. The chart at right sums up some of their important characteristics.

Widely-adapted penstemons

There are several penstemons that can be grown over a wide range of climatic conditions, from USDA Zones 3 to 9. Except where noted, all tolerate average garden conditions, as long as the drainage is good. Perhaps the most popular is pineleaf penstemon (*Penstemon pinifolius*). This compact plant is well suited for planting along the front edge of a border. Its foliage, which grows between 4 in. and 10 in. tall, is tidy and attractive year-round. The orange-scarlet flowers look lovely combined with yellow-and-red flowered gaillardias, yellow Dahlberg daisies and single, yellow marigolds.

The main bloom of pineleaf penstemon comes in early June, but it bears a few flowers over a long period. Native to the Chihuahuan desert, where moisture is unpredictable, it has adapted by blooming when the rains come, often in autumn. In the garden, it flowers as long as water is available.

Foxglove penstemon (*P. digitalis*), native to moderately-moist prairies and grasslands, is another widely-adapted species. In flower, it forms a clump up to 1 ft. wide and 1½ ft. tall. The ¾-in.-long, bright white flowers soften nearby, strong colors. I have used it successfully near peonies, late irises and early daylilies. The leaves of 'Husker Red' turn a deep, ruby red with the first cool weather of fall. Because its stems remain quite leafy even after bloom, it lends interest to the border all winter.

Of the large, red-flowered penstemons, sharkshead penstemon (*P. barbatus*) is the most readily available. It tolerates cold winters as well as the heat and humidity of the South. Reaching about 3 ft. tall, this species has bright scarlet flowers that appear

A Selection of Penstemons

Species or cultivar	Bloom time (in Colorado)	Flower Color	Region(s) of adaptability*
Widely-adapted			
Penstemon smallii	mid-May	lavender	everywhere
P. pinifolius	early June	red-orange	everywhere
P. digitalis	early June	white	everywhere
P. barbatus	early June	red	everywhere
P. eatonii	mid-June	red	SW, N (Zones 4 -10)
P. murrayanus	mid-June	deep coral	SW, Mid-W, SE (Zone 5)
P. gloxinioides	mid-June	blue, pink, white, red, purple	grow as annual; SE, SW
P. campanulatus	mid-June	purple, pink, red	SE, SW, annual elsewhere
Dryland			
P. nitidus	late April	turquoise-blue	SW, Mid-W, NE, arid W, arid PNW
P. angustifolius	early May	sky-blue	SW, Mid-W, NE, arid W, arid PNW
P. secundiflorus	May	lavender to pink	SW, Mid-W, NE, arid W, arid PNW
P. caryi	May	blue	SW, NE, Mid-W, W, PNW
P. parryi	May	pink	SW, Mid-W, reliable only south of Zone 5
P. superbus	May	pink	SW, reliable only south of Zone 5
P. caespitosus	mid-May	bright blue	SW, NE, Mid-W, W
P. crandallii	mid-May	bright blue	SW, NE, Mid-W, W
P. cyananthus	late May	blue	SW, NE, Mid-W, W, PNW
P. glaber	early June	blue	SW, NE, Mid-W, W, PNW
P. baccharifolius	early June– July; August	red	Zones 5-10
P. ambiguus	June	white w/ pink	SW, Mid-W, SE
P. palmeri	mid June-July	white or pink	SW, Mid-W,W, SE, NE
Rock garden			
P. procerus subsp. formosus	May	deep blue	everywhere
P. hirsutus 'Pygmaeus'	mid-May	lavender to pink	everywhere
P. davidsonii	mid-May	lavender	NE, NW, Mid-W
P. rupicola	mid-May	pink	NW, NE, Mid-W
P. fruticosus	mid-May	lavender	NE, NW, Mid-W
Prairie and meadow garden			
P. grandiflorus	May	lav., pink or white	everywhere
P. cobaea	early June	white or pink	everywhere
P. strictus	June	deep blue	everywhere

*KEY: NE = Northeast; Mid-At = Mid-Atlantic; SE = Southeast; SC = Southcentral; SW= Southwest; Mid-W = Midwest; W = West; PNW = Pacific Northwest

in late May, like a bright exclamation point announcing the vivid colors of summer. The flowers resemble a shark's head—the upper lip of the flower extends well beyond the mouth, and the lower lip is folded back under. Sharkshead penstemon is fairly long-lived in the garden—from two to five years—and appreciates dry soil. I have grown *P. barbatus* in very hot locations, even next to a south-facing brick wall. 'Schooley's Yellow' is a lovely yellow-flowered variety.

Bright red flowers are fairly unusual, so the red penstemons are much in demand for the daring designer. *P. eatonii* looks much like *P. barbatus* but has tubular flowers and blooms a little later. *P. murrayanus* is less available, but lovely—a stately, architectural plant that grows up to 6 ft. tall, and bears beautiful, deep coral flowers, set off against dramatic, gray-blue leaves.

Among the most widely-grown penstemons in America today is a dwarf strain of hybrids that are sold under a

Hybrid penstemons such as 'Garnet' (shown at right), a crimson cultivar, and the purple-and-white mixture (shown above), can offer gardeners an expanded range of colors and garden adaptability.

Penstemons look attractive massed in a border. Here, a collection of hybrids is set off by pink geraniums and petunias growing above a trellis of roses.

confusing number of cultivar names. These include 'Rose Elf', 'Prairie Fire', 'Prairie Sunset', 'Prairie Dusk', *P. barbatus* 'Nana Praecox', *P. barbatus* 'Viehmeier Hybrids' and 'Flathead Lake Hybrids'. Most of these are compact replicas of *P. barbatus*, growing 12 in. to 24 in. tall, but with flowers in shades of pastel pink, purple and red. They tolerate typical perennial garden soils far better than most penstemon species. They rarely come true from seed, but all of the hybrids

produce enough basal shoots to provide lots of cuttings.

Perhaps the most promising new development in the genus is a strain widely sold as 'Hyacinth-Flowered' penstemon. These giant-flowered, dwarf plants bloom for much of the summer. The flowers, 2 in. or more wide, and equally long, come in an astonishing range of hard-candy colors—grape-purple, red-hot scarlets, spicy violets and ice-blue lavenders. They can live two to four years in the garden.

A rich variety of penstemons from the mesic (moderately-moist) areas of Mexico are well-suited for gardens. Though not as cold-hardy as the other widely-adapted penstemons I've described, they are superb grown as perennials in regions with only light frosts. Or grow them as annuals anywhere. The two most frequently grown Mexican penstemons are *P. gloxinioides* and *P. campanulatus*, along with a broad range of their hybrids. All produce a neat tuft of glossy, green basal foliage and a constant succession of trumpet-shaped blooms on stems that are 2 ft. or so tall. Their flowers, some of the largest in the genus, range from bright, cherry red with a white throat, to dusky purple and screaming crimson. North of Zone 7, they behave as annuals, blooming throughout the first season.

P. smallii, an attractive, 2-ft.-tall plant with cute, fat, lavender-to-white flowers, is a woodlander. It will grow in part-shade or full sun and is one of the best to grow in moist climates, like those of the eastern and southeastern United States.

Dryland penstemons

Many penstemons are especially adapted to, and in fact, require, dry conditions. With increasing interest in xeriscape gardens, these penstemons should come into their own. Many of these dryland plants are touchy to grow in eastern or southeastern climates, which have higher humidity and more rainfall than our annual average of 14 in. In my clay soil, I need to water them only infrequently.

Here in Colorado, the dryland penstemon season starts with *P. nitidus*. In late April, its rosette of thick, fleshy, silvery leaves sends up 8-in. to 10-in. stalks of lovely turquoise-blue flowers. They bloom for as long as three weeks, and before they are finished, they are joined by lilac penstemon (*P. secundiflorus*), a 2-ft.- to 3-ft.-tall species with large flowers in shades of lavender to pink, and *P. angustifolius*, a 12-in.- to 14-in.-tall plant with sky-blue flowers.

In May, the mat-forming *P. caespitosus* and *P. crandallii* spread through the garden like blue pools, 1 ft. or more across. The darker, clear blue flowers of *P. caryi* also open in May, followed by those of *P. glaber* and *P. cyananthus* in June. All of these species have medium-green, glossy foliage, and range in height from 1 ft. to 2 ft. tall.

A truly magnificent dryland plant is *P. palmeri*, growing a stately 4 ft. to 7 ft. tall. Blooming in mid-June, its honey-scented, 2-in.-long, fat, white or pink flowers invite bumblebees. The serrate, glaucous, basal leaves form an attractive, foot-wide clump. It fends for itself so well that the Idaho Highway Department uses it in roadside wildflower plantings, where it makes fabulous displays while requiring no attention other than a gravel mulch.

The phlox-flowered penstemon (*P. ambiguus*) does best in well-aerated, sandy soils, similar to its native habitat in the southern Great Plains and Great Basin and the Southwest. Its airy flowers, a glistening white and pink, appear in June and sometimes through the end of summer. In my garden, the plants have never produced the beautiful, symmetrical domes of flowers seen in the wild, but perhaps with a sandier soil I'll succeed.

There are several wonderful penstemons native to the dry climates of Arizona and New Mexico, including *P. parryi* and *P. superbus*, which have luminous pink flowers and grow 14 in. to 30 in. tall. They are not reliably winter-hardy here, but if you garden south of USDA Zone 5, try them as well as the excellent *P. baccharifolius*, an evergreen penstemon with very becoming leaves and Christmas-red flowers.

Penstemons for rock gardens

There are a number of beautiful penstemons small enough for rock gardens, where gritty soil and a sloping surface provide the sharp drainage they need. I irrigate these penstemons as I do the rest of my rock garden. A mulch of ¼-in.- to ¾-in. gravel helps prevent diseases. Never mulch any penstemons with organic materials.

Almost everywhere in the United States, a beautiful rock garden plant is *P. hirsutus* 'Pygmaeus'. This selection, which comes relatively true from seed, displays lavender flowers, white within the mouth, on 4-in. to 6-in. stems and deep purple winter foliage. 'Pygmaeus' is easy to grow and often self-sows. Some gardeners have reported sugar-pink versions of this flower.

Equally easy and rewarding, in any

Penstemon davidsonii var. *menziesii*, is an excellent, low-growing, shrubby plant, well suited to rock gardens.

climate where sufficient water and shade from strong sun can be provided, are the dwarf forms of *P. procerus*. This plant is so variable that I have stopped growing it from seed, and instead grow only cutting-propagated clones. I have a lovely form of the subspecies *formosus*, with basal rosettes scarcely an inch in diameter and tiny, deep blue flowers in dense clusters.

P. davidsonii, from the Cascade Mountains of Oregon and Washington and the northern Sierra Nevadas of California, is one of the very best shrubby types, all of which form small, evergreen bushes under 24 in. tall and bear large flowers. This widely-adapted species, with its fat, pleated, lavender flowers and tiny leaves, has become indispensible for rock gardeners. It grows quite flat to the ground, spreading 1 ft. or more in diameter. Several excellent selections are available.

P. rupicola is perhaps the most coveted rock garden species. The blue-gray leaves of this shrubby plant are rounded and slightly toothed. The flowers of the species are pure pink; 'Albus' has white flowers. In nature, this species grows high in the mountains, in rock or rock screes. Because it demands winter shade and prefers cool nights throughout the summer, growing it has proved the frustration of many excellent gardeners. A recent introduction by Siskiyou Rare Plant Nursery, 'Diamond Lake', whose flowers are a little more lavender than the species, seems to be much easier to please.

P. fruticosus is a wonderful shrubby species for a large rock garden. It grows about 8 in. to 12 in. tall, and is covered with lavender flowers well set off against its dark green foliage. There are also several good selections. It's a fairly long-lived plant when it's happy; many growers have had it ten years or more.

Penstemons for prairie and meadow gardens

For prairie or meadow culture, *P. grandiflorus*, *P. cobaea*, and *P. strictus* are all excellent plants that withstand windy, open sites. They range from 2½ ft. to 4 ft. tall, with large flowers of lavender, pink or white; white or pink, and deep blue, respectively. They need sun, good drainage and regular moisture. A friend in Wisconsin combines blue flax, yellow-orange wallflower and *P. grandiflorus* for a stunning show. A lovely white selection of *P. grandiflorus*, 'Prairie Snow', should be available soon.

Propagating penstemons

If you want to keep a particular penstemon in your garden for a long time, you must regularly propagate it. Penstemons

Rock gardens provide a perfect setting for displaying and growing the large number of penstemons native to this habitat. Here, the salmon flowers of a hybrid penstemon (right, foreground) stand out against the gray foliage of *Calocephalis brownii* and the pink flowers of *Nemesia capensis*.

Photos: Jerry Pavia

are among the easiest and most rewarding plants to grow from seed. You can buy seed or collect it, an easy task since the plants produce a large amount. The seed capsules have sharp points, so if you wait to collect the seed until the capsules open, you'll save yourself the pain of getting stuck by them. At that time, tip the stems upside down over an envelope and the seeds will fall out. I sow the chaff and seed together, but if you are starting them in a more sterile, greenhouse environment, remove as much of the chaff as possible, as it might carry a fungus.

Store all freshly-harvested penstemon seed for at least six weeks before sowing it. Penstemon seeds remain viable for a long time, even under ordinary household conditions.

I have started penstemons indoors under lights, and outdoors in open frames, using virtually the same method as I do for all my perennials. I sow the seed in 4-in. pots in equal parts peat/perlite growing medium and sand, topped with a thin layer of aquarium gravel. I bottom water the pots and then put them in sand frames outside, or indoors under lights. My sand frames are nothing more than four 8-in.-wide boards nailed into a frame and filled with about 2 in. of a rough-textured play sand.

I sow seed on New Year's Day. Many of the species in the sand frame germinate the first spring; the rest may germinate up to a year later. I overwinter those that don't germinate in the frames, uncovered. Indoors under lights, many penstemons sprout within three weeks, without exposure to cold. If they haven't germinated by then, I move them into the sand frame until they do.

Cuttings are a ready method of propagating the shrubby and the mat-forming penstemons. If you have a desirable shrubby penstemon, experiment with cuttings, since many of these plants live fewer than five years in the garden.

Cuttings 1 in. to 3 in. long seem to root well if taken about four to six weeks after the plants bloom. Remove the leaves from the bottom half of the cutting and stick it into a flat or pot of damp sand or perlite, or into the seed-starting medium recommended earlier, which doesn't require as frequent watering. For faster rooting and a higher success rate, dip the lower part of the cutting into a rooting hormone first. I root cuttings outdoors in a shady spot, keeping them moist and in a humid environment. When you see new growth on the cutting, gently tug on it. If you feel resistance, roots have formed, and you can gently remove it from the flat and pot it up. If roots haven't formed, stick the cutting

Dwarf hybrids of *P. barbatus*, such as 'Elfin Pink', tolerate rich, irrigated soils better than most penstemons do. The flowers of this hybrid complement those of a blue marguerite behind.

RESOURCES

To learn more about penstemons, join the American Penstemon Society. Write to Ann Bartlett, Secretary, 1569 S. Holland Ct., Lakewood, CO 80232. The yearly membership fee of $10 includes two annual bulletins, a seed exchange and round robin letters among members.

The author recommends the following mail-order sources of penstemons.

Plants:

Colorado Alpines, P.O. Box 2708, Avon, CO 81620. 303-949-6464. Catalog $2.00.

Lamb Nurseries, E. 101 Sharp Ave., Spokane, Washington 99202. Catalog $1.00.

Plants of the Southwest, 930 Baca St., Santa Fe, New Mexico 87501. 505-983-1548. Catalog $1.50.

Siskiyou Rare Plant Nursery, 2825 Cummings Rd., Medford, OR 97501. 503-772-6846. Catalog $2.00 refundable with first order.

Seeds:

American Penstemon Society, (address above.)

American Rock Garden Society, P.O. Box 67, Millwood, NY 10546. Membership, $25.

Rocky Mountain Rare Plants, P.O. Box 200483, Denver, CO 80220. Catalog $1.00.

back in the medium until they do. I frequently leave my cuttings in the frames over winter, where they continue to root. If you live in a humid climate, you may need to periodically drench the cuttings with an anti-fungal solution.

Penstemons that form basal rosettes of leaves usually form additional rosettes. These can easily be cut off, with their attached roots, and planted. You can encourage more offsets to form by cutting off flowering stalks immediately after the plants bloom.

Cultural tips

Penstemons are short-lived. Many even behave like biennials in the garden, overwintering as rosettes, sending up a beautiful display of flowers in spring and then dying. To my way of thinking, they are worth growing even for one year's display.

Many causes of their demise have been debated. Older plants may be less resistant to overwatering than younger ones; a black spot fungus is known to attack penstemons grown far from their arid homes. It looks like its name suggests and can be treated with a fungicide drench. Swollen, twisted, deformed stems are probably an indicator of pittosporum pit scale, a white or tan scale. While a systemic insecticide might be effective, it will probably burn the foliage badly if applied in hot weather. Some devoted penstemon growers swab off the wax-coated scale bodies with alcohol. If your plants are large enough, cut off the affected stems and dispose of them. You can also destroy the tiny crawlers of this scale when they appear in early spring with three applications of a contact insecticide, such as Isotox, sprayed seven to ten days apart.

The best way to extend the lives of your penstemons is to avoid overwatering them. If you live in a climate with more than 25 in. of annual precipitation, particularly if most of that falls as rain, consider growing penstemons in a mix that is at least half gravel. I have friends who successfully grow penstemons in beds of pure sand, spread up to 10 in. deep over the existing soil, and another who grows Western penstemons in a mix of pea gravel and sand.

The genus *Penstemon* is perfect for the gardener who wants to thoroughly explore a plant group. If you try to grow all the penstemons, you'll soon find yourself developing new gardening skills and new gardens. □

Gwen Kelaidis, an avid gardener in Denver, Colorado, edits the Bulletin of The American Penstemon Society.

Yarrows

Aromatic perennials for beauty and variety

The gray foliage and whitish buds of most yarrows make them good companions to richly-colored flowers. Here, 'Coronation Gold' yarrow is an effective background to the deep purple blossoms of salvia.

'Moonshine' is one of the best of the yarrows, and arguably one of the finest plant introductions in recent years. This variety is more compact than others—sulphur yellow flowers and handsome foliage come on 2-ft. plants that can easily fit into small garden spaces.

The well-named 'Paprika' is an outstanding red-and-yellow bicolor cultivar of common yarrow. Yellow-centered flowers open a very pale, pink-tinged ivory, deepening to a spicy red. To keep common yarrow vigorous, cut it back after flowering and divide it regularly.

Photos: top, Thomas E. Eltzroth; below, Pamela Harper

by Allan M. Armitage

At the time of writing this, I am up to my chin in yarrow. As a professor of horticulture, I wear numerous hats. Currently, I am conducting research on the suitability of certain perennials for use in commercial field production of cut flowers. One of these is yarrow. As my helpers and I measure the size of the flower heads and the length of the cut stems, we ponder their poetic names, such as 'Sawa Sawa', 'Wenderstein', 'The Pearl' and 'Parker's Gold'. All the while, my nose is running, my eyes are watering, and I am sneezing. I suppose I should expect this from a genus where one of the species is known as sneezewort (*A. ptarmica*).

After reading this, you might feel that I dislike members of the genus *Achillea*, but that is not the case. I am also an avid gardener, and I admire the variety, beauty, grandeur and reliability of this tough family of plants. Although approximately 100 species are known, only about a dozen are in cultivation, and even fewer are available in the trade. Yarrows are a diverse group whose members range from low-growing species such as silky yarrow (*A. clavennae*) and woolly yarrow (*A. tomentosa*) to tall growers such as fern-leaf yarrow (*A. filipendulina*) and 'Coronation Gold' yarrow. The taller forms usually have yellow flowers, but a rainbow of hues may be found in the cultivars and hybrids of common yarrow (*A. millefolium*).

Most yarrows share certain characteristics. All have alternate or basal leaves, which are usually either deeply toothed or divided. A notable exception is my friend sneezewort, which has entire leaves. Flowers are typically borne in dense heads called corymbs.

If such botanical jargon puts you to sleep, take a whiff of the foliage. The unique savory aroma of most yarrows will awaken you. This aromatic quality is one of the identifying characteristics of the genus.

Range and care

Gardeners over much of the country can grow yarrow because of its wide range of temperature tolerance. Some species will grow as far north as northern Ontario, in USDA Zone 3, and as far south as central Florida, in Zone 8. Most species are native to Europe and therefore tolerate cold winters better than hot summers—a trait that can limit their hardiness in southern climates.

Yarrows grow easily without much care. Full sun and well-drained soil are just about their only requirements. Shade causes tall species to be taller and short species to be loose and lanky. Don't give yarrows heavy doses of fertilizer, particularly nitrogen—overfeeding also results in lanky, sprawling plants.

How to use yarrows

Yarrows are easy to use in the garden. Many have gray-tinged foliage which provides a softening foil to surrounding bright splashes of color. The deep yellow forms are particularly attractive combined with the blue balloon flower (*Platycodon grandiflorus*) or as a

---

Yarrow (*Achillea* spp.)

- Hardy perennial; typical plant habit is a basal rosette of gray, finely-divided, aromatic foliage.

- Flower stems grow 4 in. to 4 ft. tall, depending on species; most garden cultivars reach 1 ft. to 3 ft. tall.

- Blooms in late spring and summer; flowers are borne in flat heads at stem ends; colors are predominantly shades of yellow, also white, red, pink, lilac, salmon, peach.

- Full sun, well-drained soil of ordinary fertility, regular moisture.

- Hardy in USDA Zones 3-9 (-40°F-30°F).

- Tough, reliable plants for perennial borders. Use shorter species in rock gardens. Excellent cut flower; dries well.

---

foreground to the classic spires of foxglove (*Digitalis purpurea*). If you feel bold, combine sulphur-yellow *A.* × 'Moonshine' with a deep red *Cosmos sulphureus*, tempered with some other gray-foliage plant such as lamb's-ears (*Stachys byzantina*) or annual dusty miller (*Centaurea cineraria*). When using the non-yellow forms of *A. millefolium*, take into consideration the plant's tendency to roam—otherwise common yarrow will be as common as its name suggests.

The cut-flower qualities of yarrows are legendary, particularly the tall, yellow-flowered species. However, it

is important that flowers be fully open before they are cut, otherwise they rapidly decline. The yellow forms can be air-dried—they'll even dry standing in a vase of water—and they make long-lasting additions to bouquets. The colored forms of common yarrow typically don't last as long—a vase life of less than one week is not unusual. They can be air-dried successfully, however.

Species and cultivars

Although approximately 100 species are known, only about a dozen are in cultivation, and even fewer are readily available. Many cultivars of the various yarrows are generally easy to find. For nurseries that offer some unusual yarrows, refer to the source list on p. 71.

Fern-leaf yarrow (*A. filipendulina*) has been a garden favorite for many years. It is unexcelled as a classic yarrow for the back of the garden or as the dominant flower in a late spring and summer border. In my garden, this yarrow grows to 4 ft. tall and associates well with plants of meadowsweet (*Filipendula palmata*) and balloon flower. Fern-leaf yarrow's green foliage is deeply divided, and plants produce dark yellow flower heads as wide as 5 in. across. They return year after year—my plants are five years old, and I expect them to live for five more. They are tough, aromatic and resistant to most insects and diseases. Occasionally, Japanese beetles chew on the foliage, but what do Japanese beetles not enjoy? Fern-leaf yarrow can be grown from seed sown in trays containing a balanced mix of peat/vermiculite or peat/perlite. Keep the trays at 70° to 72°F, and cover them with plastic or glass to increase humidity until seeds germinate, which takes two to three weeks.

Few cultivars of *A. filipendulina* are available, and in most cases differences are difficult to detect. 'Cloth of Gold' has finely-cut foliage and yellow flower heads atop 2-ft.- to 4-ft.-stems. 'Gold Plate' has deep yellow flowers on stems that usually grow 2 ft. to 3 ft. tall, but may occasionally reach 5 ft. in height. 'Parker's Variety', also known as 'Parker's Gold', is probably the most popular of the tall yarrows. The stems are strong enough to support the large flowers without staking. 'Parker's Variety' makes excellent cut flowers; the dried stems found in florist shops are usually this cultivar.

Coronation Gold yarrow (*A.* × 'Coronation Gold', is one of my favorites because of its free-flowering tendencies. This hybrid produces many basal shoots, each resulting in a 2-ft. to 3-ft. stem with a 2-in.- to 3-in.-wide, deep yellow

Illustration: Rosalind L. Wanke

flower head. The flowers are not as large, nor are the plants as tall, as cultivars of fern-leaf yarrow, but the compactness can be a virtue in small gardens, and the quantity of flowers more than makes up for their smaller size. 'Coronation Gold' produces *lots* of flowers—we routinely cut 30 to 60 stems per plant in our cut flower trials, depending on spacing. They are truly magnificent when the flowers almost completely hide the gray-green foliage—the fields are alive with the sight of yarrow. The flowers persist for eight to 12 weeks.

'Coronation Gold' is the result of a cross between fern-leaf yarrow (*A. filipendulina*) and *A. clypeolata*, a smaller, deep yellow species. When buying plants, be sure to purchase only those that have been vegetatively propagated. Seed labeled as 'Coronation Gold' will not produce seedlings like the true hybrid.

Common yarrow (*A. millefolium*) is a species that elicits feelings of enjoyment and dislike with equal fervor. Here is a plant that asks for nothing but full sun and routine drainage, that requires no fertilizing, no deadheading and no support. Plants are long-lived and reward the gardener with hundreds of colorful flowers, so that even the most black-thumbed gardener can be successful. So why do some people dislike it so? Perhaps it is because its own success has made it too plebeian for the "connoisseur" gardener. Common yarrow does move freely in the garden, but I don't consider it truly aggressive. The mat-like, dark green foliage is so deeply cut that the leaves appear to be divided into a thousand leaflets (thus the specific epithet, *millefolium*). And the flowers, white in the species, have been selected and bred to yield colors from magenta to primrose yellow. The flower heads, though small compared to the two yarrows described previously, are produced freely to form colorful colonies in late spring and summer.

In parts of the South where summer night temperatures routinely remain above 70°F, common yarrow doesn't perform as well as it does in the North. It certainly spreads freely and flowers profusely, but the high temperatures in late spring and summer result in thinner flower stems and lankier growth, and plants tend to flop. I don't grow common yarrow in my garden, but I do use many of the hybrids in our cut-flower program. They are better dried than fresh—they last only about four days as fresh flowers. Mature flowers can be dried in a well-ventilated room at 45° to 50°F.

Common yarrow is easy to propagate by division in the spring or after flowering; in fact, dividing rejuvenates plants and should be done every two years. Seed is also relatively easy to obtain and may be germinated similarly to *A. filipendulina*. If uniform color and habit is important, however, propagate by division.

Numerous cultivars of common yarrow are available. 'Cerise Queen', sometimes listed as 'Cherry Queen', is

Woolly yarrow is perfect for rock gardens where it gets the sharp drainage it requires. Everything about the plant is diminutive, from its 9-in. flower stems to its tiny, ferny leaves. This species does best where summers are mild. Elsewhere treat it as an annual.

Like other cultivars of common yarrow, 'Lilac Beauty' makes excellent dried flowers—simply hang stems of fully-opened blossoms in a cool, airy room. In the garden, the lilac flowers are set off beautifully against finely cut, deep green foliage.

still one of the best selections. It bears deep cherry-red flowers on 18-in. to 20-in. plants. 'Paprika' is a wonderful red-and-yellow bicolor which has been outstanding in our trials. The plants are vigorous, and the flowers are profuse. The widely-available 'Red Beauty' reliably produces 18-in. to 20-in. stems of crimson-red flowers. Numerous other cultivars have been placed under the flagship 'Beauty' name. 'Lilac Beauty' is the best of the group, and forms plants the same size as 'Red Beauty'. Unfortunately, it is not as easy to locate as many others. 'Rose Beauty' (sometimes called 'Roseum') and 'White Beauty' flower heavily on 18-in. to 24-in. plants.

Of the newer cultivars, I have been most impressed with those in the Galaxy series, which are results of crosses between *A. taygetea* and *A. millefolium*. The flowers are larger than those of common yarrow, and the plants' habits are slightly more upright. Selections include 'Appleblossom' ('Apfelblute'), with pink to peach-colored flowers; 'Great Expectations' ('Hoffnung', 'Hope'), with primrose-yellow blossoms; 'Salmon Beauty' ('Lachsschoenheit'), taller than others, producing salmon-colored flowers on 2-ft. to 3-ft. plants; 'The Beacon' ('Fanal') bears rich red flowers with yellow centers. All common yarrow cultivars may be cut back hard after flowering and divided to your heart's content.

A. × **'Moonshine'** has turned people's heads for decades because of the lovely sulphur-yellow flowers borne on 2-ft. plants. This hybrid, a cross between *A. taygetea* and *A. clypeolata*, was developed by the noted British nurseryman, Alan Bloom. 'Moonshine' is a smaller version of the fern-leaf yarrow, except for 'Moonshine's' grayer foliage and the primrose tint to its flower heads. The small, compact stature lends 'Moonshine' more readily to smaller gardens than do the large, fern-leaf forms. It is undoubtedly one of the finest plant introductions in recent years.

'Moonshine' isn't without problems, however. In the South, the combination of prevalent evening thunderstorms and hot, humid weather take a toll on the foliage, and numerous foliar diseases occur. In southeastern gardens, this hybrid performs best during summers of drought, but that circumstance is the exception and not the rule. In my garden I don't expect more than two years from 'Moonshine'; other gardeners treat it as an annual. This doesn't detract from its beauty—in my part of the country, 'Moonshine' simply must be handled differently from other yarrows. Cutting back the foliage

Photos: top, Pamela Harper; below, Thomas E. Eltzroth

after flowering is helpful, but the foliage is part of the pleasure of the plant in the first place. My gardening experiences in Montreal and Michigan simply did not prepare me for such 'Moonshine' hacking. This hybrid looks very nice with purple-foliaged companions such as purple loosestrife (*Lysimachia ciliata* 'Purpurea') or purple sage (*Salvia officinalis* 'Purpurescens'). Propagate 'Moonshine' from divisions in the early spring or after flowering.

Sneezewort (*A. ptarmica*) is not one of my favorites. To me, it is oversold and overrated as a garden plant and certainly as a cut flower. It is weedy or soon will be after flowering, the flowers are a nondescript muddy white — even in some of the better "double" cultivars — and I have trouble becoming enamored with any plant called sneezewort (the dried roots were used for snuff). In cooler areas such as the Northeast and Northwest, sneezewort has its place, and I have admired some lovely plantings in those areas. I have also seen its weak-stem characteristic used to advantage when plants are allowed to cascade across a walk. If used with creative discretion, sneezewort can be a pleasant addition to the garden. The finely-toothed foliage is not dissected, but entire, and leaves lack petioles (leaf stems)—two characteristics that distinguish it from other yarrows. When plants are at their best, the double, white flowers of some of the better cultivars are handsome and arresting. After flowering, however, plants tend to sprawl like a drunk on a barroom floor. Remove the spent flowers and cut the plant back so you can enjoy it again next year. In warmer parts of the country, plants may die if not cut back.

There are cultivars that are improvements on the species. Although all claim to produce double flowers, they all have a percentage of flowers that are semi-double and single, depending on the cultivar. The better types maintain a high percentage of double flowers even in warm weather.

'Angel's Breath' is an old cultivar with many ball-shaped, double, white flowers on 20-in. to 24-in. stems. 'Ballerina' is a relatively recent introduction whose dwarf habit (it's only 8 in. to 12 in. tall) is welcome. White, double flowers are produced late spring through summer. This variety is recommended for southern gardeners. 'The Pearl' is the best known and most popular cultivar. It's better than 'Angel's Breath' and bears many double, white flowers on 2-ft. stems.

Propagate *A. ptarmica* and its culti-

The primrose yellow flowers of 'Hoffnung' (sometimes listed as 'Great Expectations' or 'Hope') make a pleasing and restful combination with ornamental grasses and the light lavender spikes of veronica.

SOURCES

The following mail-order nurseries all offer at least half a dozen of the yarrows mentioned in this article.

Bluestone Perennials, 7211 Middle Ridge Rd., Madison, OH 44057, 216-428-7535. Catalog free. Offers 10 varieties.

Carroll Gardens, P.O. Box 310, 444 E. Main St., Westminster, MD 21157, 301-848-5422. Catalog $2.00 refundable. Offers 24 species and cultivars.

Garden Place, P.O. Box 388, Mentor, OH 44061-0388, 216-259-5252. Catalog $1. Offers 12 varieties.

Andre Viette Farm & Nursery, Route 1, Box 16-FG, Fishersville, VA 22939. Catalog $2. Offers eight varieties.

Wayside Gardens, 1 Garden Ln., Hodges, SC 29695-0001, 800-845-1124. Catalog free. Offers seven varieties.

White Flower Farm, Rte. 63, Litchfield, CT 06759-0050, 800-888-7756. Catalog free. Offers six varieties.

vars by division or from seed, which is available for the species and some of the cultivars. Division is essential to maintain the integrity (for example, fully-double flowers or strong stems) of the better forms.

Woolly yarrow (*A. tomentosa*) is a handsome plant for rock gardens or for crawling over stone edgings. The foliage is wonderful, particularly in early spring when the long, grayish hairs surrounding each leaf give the plant a truly "woolly" appearance. As the plant matures, it forms a mat of gray-green foliage, although the gray sheen of the hairs becomes less conspicuous. The sulphur-yellow flowers, borne on 9-in. stems, are similar to, but smaller than, those of 'Moonshine'. They appear in late spring and continue well into the summer. Unfortunately, plants frustrate gardeners in locales with hot, humid summers (south of USDA Zone 6). The foliage tends to "melt out," and plants decline in the heat. Excellent drainage and partial shade help to alleviate the problem. However, some gardeners, like me, enjoy the spring growth and early summer performance so much that we treat it as a hardy annual, replacing plants in the fall.

Cultivars do not differ from the species or each other a great deal, but may have brighter flowers or more aggressive growth habits. 'Aurea' (*A. tomentosa* var. *aurea*) has golden yellow flowers on 3-in. to 8-in. stems. 'King Edward VIII' is the most popular; it bears pale yellow flowers atop 10-in. to 12-in. plants. 'Moonlight' is even taller (10 in. to 18 in.), but otherwise is similar to the species. Propagate the species and 'Aurea' from seed, the others by division. □

Allan Armitage is a professor of horticulture at the University of Georgia, Athens, GA.

Photo: Pamela Harper

Primrose Primer

Early bloom to brighten moist, shady corners

by Sydney Eddison

Sometimes the most compelling reason for growing a plant is sentiment. When my English mother was growing up, primroses abounded in the fields and hedgerows of her native Devonshire. To her, primroses meant home, and her de-scriptions of them were so vivid that, as a child, I had a clear picture of the plants in my mind's eye. Even so, I was unprepared for the impact when, many years later, I saw them for the first time in their natural habitat.

They were common English primroses (*Primula vulgaris*), with blossoms the color of an autumn moon, and a light, sweet scent. Enthralled, I dug a single plant and took it home, giving little thought to whether the purloined primrose would survive in Connecticut. Fortunately, it did, and now, 25 years later, I have a garden full of primroses to show for it.

Even if you're not a sentimental Anglo-phile, I recommend primroses highly for the early color they bring to moist, shady places in the garden. In April, when most perennials are no more than sprouts, the

Primroses enliven the drab days of early spring in author Eddison's garden (above).

primroses along my woodland path are in full bloom. Their abundant blossoms completely hide the young leaves and form shallow mounds of yellow, cream and white; pink and rose; soft blue and deep blue; royal purple and rich red.

This amazing array of shades and hues is largely the work of centuries of plant breeding. In nature, the range is more limited, but no less lovely. And, with more than 500 species, the genus *Primula* offers plants of many sizes and shapes. Some species are so tiny that to appreciate them you have to get down on your hands and knees. Others rise on 4-ft. stalks. Individual flowers can be as small as a baby's fingernail or as large as a silver dollar, borne singly or in clusters. Even the clusters come in different configurations—tight, globe shapes; nodding, mop-like heads; hyacinthine spires or elegant tiers of flowers arranged one above the other.

Wild primroses are scattered all over the Northern Hemisphere from the peaks of the Himalayas and Rockies to the damp meadows of western Europe; from the Swiss Alps to the woodlands of Japan. That these far-flung habitats differ considerably is an important factor to bear in mind when selecting primroses for a garden. For example, mountain dwellers that make their homes in crevices high above the timberline demand specific conditions that are difficult to reproduce elsewhere. This group of primrose prima donnas includes most of the American natives, inhabitants of the high western mountains.

I have rock-gardening friends who raise these difficult primroses in pots in alpine houses—sort of grownup cold frames allowing for careful control of temperature and air circulation. But I'm afraid I haven't the time for that. There are, however, other primulas that can more easily be raised out of doors. For New England, the most forgiving are those that in the wild inhabit damp meadows beneath the tree line and cool, moist woodlands. What they miss from home—the ground moisture, the cool air and the frequently overcast skies—can be approximated in the garden. They don't enjoy our heat, humidity and inadequate summer rainfall, but they survive and even prosper.

My primrose garden owes its development as much to my fascination with water as to a passion for primroses. The site was typical of abandoned New England farmland: a scrap of rocky pasture that had reverted to woods, bounded by dilapidated stone walls. Its only unique features were a tiny stream fed by spring rains and runoff, and a tree-filled pond. By the spring of 1978, after 18 years of hacking through the overgrowth to create gardens around the house, I was ready to tackle the stream and pond behind the barn.

After clearing the debris from the

'Hose-in-Hose' primroses, with their distinctive double blossom (bottom left), thrive next to Eddison's stream (top). The simple blossoms of the common English primrose, *Primula vulgaris* (bottom right), balance on thin, fuzzy stems that rise above rosettes of crisp, heavily crinkled leaves.

stream, I began to line the banks with large rocks to keep the water in a single channel, adding soil to the pockets between stones. Then I thought about plants. My English primrose had flourished in the shade of an old apple tree; the stream banks seemed the perfect place for its progeny. Moreover, a generous friend offered me half a dozen 'Hose-in-Hose' primroses (shown above). A "sport," or mutation, of the common *P.* × *polyantha*, 'Hose-in-Hose' has a double blossom, the normal green calyx replaced with another flower. These vigorous plants are still the backbone of my primrose garden.

I put in the first primroses in early April. The conditions seemed ideal. Water was plentiful; the sunlight was bright but not too hot, and poured through the leafless trees. The primroses prospered. By mid-May, though, the stream was a mere trickle, the pond was shrinking and the trees were leafing out. A month later, the stream and pond were dry and the shade so complete that I knew the primroses would be starved for light.

If I had taken a good look into the woods the previous summer, I would have foreseen this. In a woodland dominated by leafy, shallow-rooted sugar maples, very little grows on the forest floor—maple saplings, a few struggling spice bushes, clumps of the indomitable Christmas fern. Few other plants can make do with so little light and so much root competition.

Something had to be done. So, I prevailed upon my husband to employ the chainsaw ruthlessly. He cut down young maples, limbed ones too big to remove and cleared the pond of trees. His efforts had one immediate consequence. Suddenly given light, long-dormant weed seeds germinated and soon weeds carpeted the area. After several years, I finally got them under control with mulch and by planting ferns to shade the bare earth. I still need to clean them out at least once a year.

Today, the light in the garden can best be described as blotchy shade. In early morning, the whole garden is in forest shadow. There are patches of full sun throughout the morning, but by early afternoon sunlight streams through the trees. From

Photos: facing page, top and bottom right above, Viki Ferreniea; bottom left above, Staff

P. sibthorpii's fragile-looking blossoms make the plant appear delicate, but it has a relatively husky constitution.

P. juliae emerges from underground stolons and forms a patch of deep-green foliage. The purple-flowered hybrid shown here is 'Wanda'.

Perched on sturdy stems, polyanthus blooms run the gamut from pastel tints to shades of intense, velvety richness.

The round mass of little flowers in the umbel of P. denticulata begins to bloom at ground level, then rises on the stem to its full 18-in. height.

Tiny flowers and large calyxes are characteristic of cowslips, P. veris. Widespread as a wildflower, cowslips are a favorite in England.

The 12-in.-long stems of P. sieboldii carry loose clusters of irregularly shaped flowers. The petals can be delicately incised or notched.

midafternoon it stripes the garden as it passes behind the remaining trees before sinking below the hills. The primroses seem satisfied, wilting in the sun's heat but recovering in subsequent shadiness.

Improving the soil was even more critical than providing adequate light. Humus-rich, moisture-retentive soil plays a vital part in growing primroses, especially in southern New England. Here, we must compensate for the sun's heat and the absence of the regular, gentle rain that they receive in their native habitat. A moist soil helps, as does a mulch of chopped leaves. (Whole leaves, especially maple leaves, tend to mat down; I cut mine up with a rotary lawn mower.) The mulch keeps the soil cool, retards evaporation, discourages weeds and eventually decomposes to improve the soil.

Our woodland soil—shallow, dry and netted with the water-demanding roots of maples—leaves a lot to be desired. Wherever I plant, I add peat moss and compost. This organic matter holds water like a sponge and harbors bacteria that turn the compost into plant food. In rocky, root-choked areas, I lay a course or two of logs, one on top of the other, and fill in with old hay, manure, compost, peat moss and topsoil. Started in the summer, such beds are ready to plant the following spring. The organic material may not have all broken down, but that doesn't seem to matter as long as the top 3 in. or so is soft and crumbly.

Despite the limitations of our site and climate, a remarkable number of primrose species thrive here. I grow about a dozen and feel that I haven't even scratched the surface. Joining The American Rock Garden Society and The American Primrose Society (for their addresses, see facing page) opened my eyes to the breadth of the primrose world. Their publications are gold mines of information and so are their members, who are as generous with plants as they are with tips on culture. I now try a new species or two every year.

Primrose species are so varied and their numbers so great that they have been divided into subgenera and 37 "sections." (Catalogs seldom mention sections, but plant-society publications and some books do.) These groupings are based on geographic criteria, genetic similarities and shared physical characteristics. Many of the distinctions are arcane to me, but I find it useful to know that the plants in any one section usually have similar cultural preferences.

The primroses I grow fall into one of two simpler categories: woodlanders or water-lovers. Woodlanders need a moisture-retentive soil and some form of protection from the hot sun. While they appreciate supplementary water during periods of drought, they can survive if the

P. japonica have self-sown happily in the clay soil bordering Eddison's small pond. Rings of flowers rise one above another on a single stem.

soil has been well prepared and well mulched. For the water-lovers, however, a constant source of moisture is critical. Without it they will die.

Most of my primroses are woodlanders, many of them from the Primula section. *P. vulgaris* and the 'Hose-in-Hose' primroses belong to this section, as do four other European primroses I recommend highly: *P. sibthorpii, P. juliae, P. veris* and *P. × polyantha* (photos, facing page). Though not easy to find in nursery catalogs, *P. sibthorpii,* which is a native of the Caucasus and a subspecies of *vulgaris,* is worth seeking out for its exceptionally early shell-pink flowers, which open in March in my garden. Hybrids of *P. juliae,* another Caucasian native, are readily available at many nurseries and garden centers. The most popular is the purple-flowered 'Wanda'.

In England, cowslips (*P. veris*) are almost as much loved as the common primrose, although Americans may have difficulty understanding the attraction—the flowers are small and dominated by the puffy calyxes in which they are clasped. *P. veris* is among the most widespread of all primroses in the wild, appearing from Europe to Mongolia. I plant these en masse on a bank out of the direct sun. The many varieties of polyanthus primroses, on the other hand, are sumptuous. Developed from naturally occurring hybrids of *P. vulgaris* and *P. veris,* they boast huge heads of colorful flowers, each bloom the size of a silver dollar.

Two Asian species do well in my woodland garden. The first, *P. denticulata,* is commonly called the "drumstick" primrose. It bears a globe-shaped umbel of flowers in shades of lilac-pink, lavender and rosy purple. There is also a lovely white form. *P. denticulata,* from the section Denticulata, is easy to acquire and

very easy to grow. Though it has the same preferences as other woodlanders, it is more tolerant of dry conditions and yet perfectly at home in positions that would suit the water-lovers.

The second Asian, *P. sieboldii,* which comes from Japan and belongs to the Cortusoides section, is also easy to find and grow. It withstands dry conditions by going dormant—the leaves completely dis-

appear in summer and return the following spring. Flowering in mid- to late May here, *P. sieboldii* ranges in color between bold magenta-pinks and pale orchid-pinks. There is a particularly beautiful white cultivar suitably named 'The Bride'.

Though my pond dries up in late June, my water-loving primroses, *P. japonica,* survive. The secret is the heavy clay soil around the pond's edge, which retains enough moisture to see them through the summer. In fact, they have self-sown with such enthusiasm that there isn't light or room enough for other water-lovers I've tried there. Nonetheless, I can't think of a more beautiful primrose than *P. japonica* (photos above). It is among the candelabra primroses, so called because of their distinctive tiers of flowers, and comes in shades of rose, pink, terra-cotta red, deep magenta and white. In my garden these plants bloom during the last two weeks in May, and by the end each 2-ft. stalk may have as many as five separate floral rings.

Maintaining my primrose garden is much less arduous than making it. Luckily, I don't need to spend much time watering; if your gardening conditions differ, this could be a more demanding chore. Virtually all primroses need the most water in the early spring when in active growth. Later, the plants can do with considerably less. In our climate, March and April are cool and the days are still short. Precipitation is frequent and in excess of 3½ in. per month, enough to give the primroses a good start.

The summer months are another story. Despite their needs being less and rainfall about the same as in the spring, the primroses are severely stressed. I can only assume that high temperatures and "welcome breezes" are the culprits. In addition, we may have periods of several dry weeks. I'd

Photos: above left, Sydney Eddison; above right, Viki Ferreniea

water during these spells, but our garden well dries up just when the primroses need it. Nevertheless, they survive.

By August, my primroses are a sight only a mother could love. *P. sieboldii* goes dormant; other species lose most of their leaves and look dog-eared. But early in the fall, the European primroses put forth a burst of new growth, becoming fresh and green once more. The amount of rain is about the same as in the summer months, but shorter days and cooler temperatures must make the difference.

One reason I can avoid watering is mulch. At the beginning of the growing season, the garden is covered with autumn's leaves. The ferns and other robust plants, such as foxgloves and Virginia Bluebells, push their way through, but the primroses have to be uncovered and I tuck the old leaves around them. Later, I top up this layer of natural mulch to a depth of at least 2 in. with shredded leaves and pine needles. Pine boughs also serve me as winter mulch. (Anything light and durable would serve the same purpose.) Applied after the ground freezes, winter mulch shades the ground and keeps it frozen. This prevents cycles of freezing and thawing, which would heave the plants out of the soil, damaging and exposing the roots to drying winds.

In my experience, primroses are not prey to pests, although aphids, red spider mites and slugs are mentioned in reference books as possible enemies. In addition, botrytis and root rot are known to attack primroses, but I've also been spared these problems. Until I installed an electric fence, however, I lost plenty of plants to foraging deer.

I have never used any commercial fertilizer on the primroses. I don't think it is necessary if the soil is full of organic matter in the first place and kept covered with decaying leaf mulch. Since I don't divide the primroses as often as the books recommend (every third year for the polyanthus hybrids), in a fit of remorse I have sometimes mulched them with manure at the beginning of the summer. I think that this does almost as much for them as division, though I've read that British gardening authority Gertrude Jekyll used to divide her primroses every year—assisted by a team of gardeners.

Even if frequent division isn't essential to the plants' vigor, it is one way of obtaining more primroses. Unfortunately, many homesick Britons and other admirers have dug primroses from the wild, as I did many years ago, and today the common English primrose has become rare in places where it was once plentiful. Wiser now, I would never again be so irresponsible. Commercially propagated primroses are readily available, and rarer species often can be obtained through membership in plant societies. Once you've got a few primroses, it's easy to propagate them by division, particularly those that are members of the Primula section.

P. vulgaris, P. veris and hybrids of *P. × polyantha,* as well as *P. denticulata,* grow into large clumps that can be separated into individual plants. I have divided these species in early spring when the rosettes are tight clusters of small leaves, but I find it easier to tease apart single rosettes during the early summer after the plants have flowered and the drier soil falls easily off the roots.

The technique couldn't be simpler. Dig up a clump, shake the loose soil off the roots and wash off the rest. Grasp a rosette on the outer edge of the mass by the stem and wiggle it until the roots come away from the others. You can divide a clump into single plants or into two or three smaller clumps. (Single divisions don't flower much, if at all, the following season.)

Newly divided clumps require protection from the sun and regular watering until they are re-established, especially if they were divided during the summer. I

When dividing primroses, dig deeply, allowing plenty of room around the roots. Then gently work apart the entwined roots of a clump.

A simple frame of lath and 1x2s protects newly transplanted primroses from direct sun.

prepare planting holes in the woodland garden by digging out a large shovelful of soil and mixing with it whatever organic matter I have on hand. The loose, crumbly soil makes it easier going for new roots. Next I put the division in at the same depth as the original clump, spread out the roots on the prepared soil, then water the plant before filling the hole with the rest of the enriched soil. Screens made of 1x2s and lath let in light, but keep off the direct sun and temper the drying winds (photo below). I leave them in place for a week or two, longer if the weather is very hot. When their leaves droop, I know the plants need a drink.

I usually replant small, single rosettes in a nursery bed prepared the same way as the holes. In addition, I cut off about half of each leaf. Reducing the surface area of the leaves conserves water. (This is unnecessary for larger clumps, which have been disturbed less and recover more quickly.) Small rosettes must be shaded and watered regularly for several weeks until a new set of leaves develops at the base of the old foliage. Plants divided in June normally produce a new rosette by August.

I've only recently grown primroses from seed, using methods suggested by The American Primrose Society. It requires time and some vigilance, and I have not always been successful. But when it works, it's rewarding—and a very cheap way to acquire plants. In small flower pots, 4 in. across and 3 in. deep, I put a ½-in. layer of pebbles for drainage, then add a soil mix of two parts Jiffy Mix Seed Starter and one part sharp builders' sand—a gritty sand with sharp facets, which promotes root growth and drains well. I tamp down the mix to within ¼ in. of the rim, thinly scatter the seeds over the surface and cover them with a thin layer of vermiculite. Then I water the pots from the bottom in a shallow dish, filling the dish with water about halfway up the sides of the pots. When the surface of the vermiculite turns dark and feels damp, the soil mix is thoroughly watered. I remove the pots and let them stand overnight, then put them outside, exposed to the weather but in shade. I also prop a window screen on concrete blocks over the pots to break the force of the rain.

I've started seeds in February and March with equally good results. By April, the seeds have germinated, and about six weeks later, soon after the first set of true leaves has developed, the seedlings are ready to transplant. I remove them in one clump, then take a section the size of a quarter and gently pull apart the tiny plants, which already have astonishing roots an inch or two long. I replant them, an inch apart, in boxes 3½ in. deep with pebbles on the bottom and filled with a mixture of equal parts garden soil, com-

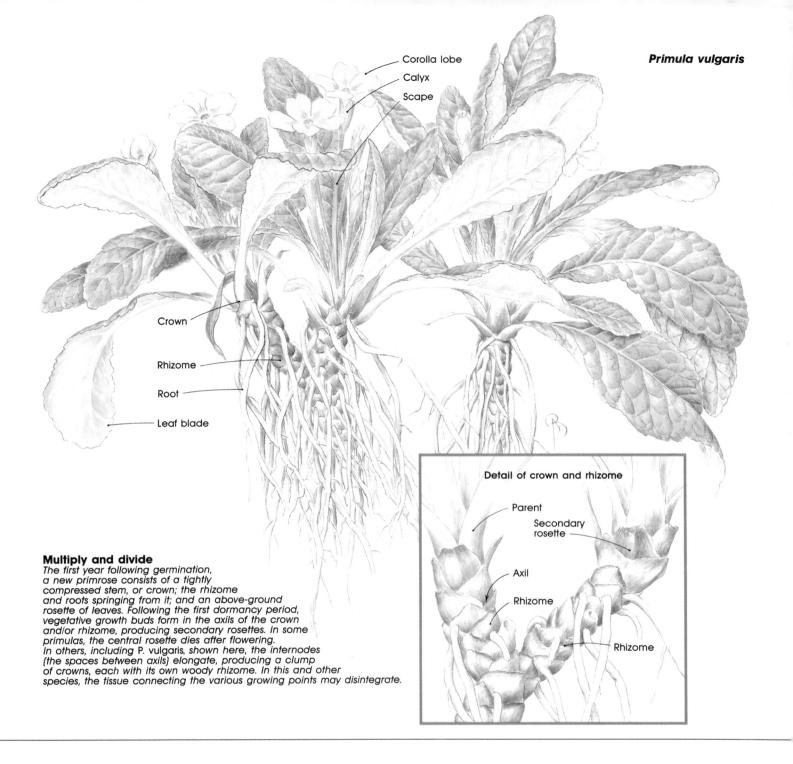

Primula vulgaris

Corolla lobe

Calyx

Scape

Crown

Rhizome

Root

Leaf blade

Detail of crown and rhizome

Parent

Secondary rosette

Axil

Rhizome

Rhizome

Multiply and divide

The first year following germination, a new primrose consists of a tightly compressed stem, or crown; the rhizome and roots springing from it; and an above-ground rosette of leaves. Following the first dormancy period, vegetative growth buds form in the axils of the crown and/or rhizome, producing secondary rosettes. In some primulas, the central rosette dies after flowering. In others, including P. vulgaris, shown here, the internodes (the spaces between axils) elongate, producing a clump of crowns, each with its own woody rhizome. In this and other species, the tissue connecting the various growing points may disintegrate.

post, peat moss and sand. Again I water from the bottom, then set the seedlings outside in the shade. This stage is tricky—they must be kept constantly moist, but the soil mix should never be soggy.

By August, I have 2-in. rosettes, ready to put out in the garden in nursery beds, shaded and watered regularly. Sometimes instead of a nursery bed I just cultivate a patch of woodland floor, incorporating the usual organic material, and plant the seedlings a couple of inches apart, in rows for easy care. In the spring, I move some of the plants elsewhere, leaving behind an irregular pattern of plants—a new addition to the permanent garden.

To grow *P. japonica* from seed, I select a rainy day in May when the plants are in full bloom, pick the color I want, gouge the chosen plant out of the clay (keeping the lump of gummy earth around the roots intact), and plop it in another hole where I want it to reseed itself. There is nothing about this method in the rule book, but it works.

I've never had a master plan for the primrose garden; in fact, very little about it has been done according to the rules. But I know now that I want a narrow wood-chip track to run around the pond, with primroses (mostly pale *P. vulgaris* in-

terspersed with a few richly colored polyanthus hybrids) spilling onto the path so that you have to pick your way through their blossoms. It is due to luck, not planning, that the woodland garden is walled in and hidden from view. In the summer, the tired primrose foliage and weed-filled pond do not detract from the rest of the garden. Yet in the spring, when little else is in bloom, coming suddenly upon the primrose path is like discovering a delicious secret. □

Sydney Eddison gardens in Newtown, Connecticut. She is a contributing editor to Fine Gardening.

The billowy, white flowers and fine-textured leaves of the perennial grass miscanthus 'Gracillimus' dramatically contrast with carefully mani-cured yews at Longwood Gardens in Kennett Square, Pennsylvania. Ornamental grasses are easy-to-grow landscape plants.

Landscaping with Ornamental Grasses

A study in movement, texture and form

by Rick Darke

My career in horticulture developed from a love of wild places. Long before I'd ever set foot in a garden or called plants by their botanical names, I felt the drama of contrasting textures, forms, colors and illumina-tion that is common to so many native landscapes. These places inspired feelings of freedom and adventure, and they conjured up notions of mystery and romance. Although the ever-present grasses were rarely my major focus, I realize now how important their unique qualities were to the appeal of the overall image. Few other plants can match the grasses' fine-textured gracefulness or the luminescent quality of their delicate flowers and seed heads. Few plants respond with such allure to a summer breeze as grasses do, and certainly the foliage and flowers of few other herbaceous perennials extend their beauty so long into winter. With proper selection of cultivars, you can grow grasses in USDA Zones 3 through 10.

All photos: Rick Darke

We all have our personal reasons for gardening. I don't want to simply imitate native landscapes, but my garden is the place where I do much of my spontaneous thinking and daydreaming; it must have the capacity to inspire. To that end, perennial ornamental grasses have become an important part of my gardening life.

A tradition of gardening with grasses

Despite all the recent fanfare about ornamental grasses, they are hardly new to American gardens. *Pennisetum*, *Miscanthus*, *Arundo* and *Erianthus* were all common in Victorian times; but they were merely magnificent curiosities, rarely integrated with the rest of the garden.

Our current fascination with grasses was sparked by a new plant palette and design philosophy imported largely from a German horticulturist, Karl Foerster (1874-1970), a devoted student of the natural landscape. Today, ornamental grasses have been linked with a naturalistic gardening style that has been referred to as the "New Romantic Landscape" or the "New American Garden." With its emphasis on grasses and less regimented designs, the style is certainly more romantic than the lawns and foundation plantings it eschews. But since it borrows so heavily from Foerster, it seems inappropriate to call it "Amercan." Rather, the style and plants of the "New American Garden" should be inspired by our landscape and culture. In this, grasses can play an important role.

The fine-textured foliage of purple needlegrass is balanced by the bold orange of California poppies.

Special qualities of ornamental grasses

Ornamental grasses are distinct from other perennials. Grasses are usually finer textured, with a strong linear effect that results from a parallel arrangement of narrow leaf blades. To take best advantage of these characteristics, grasses should be visually balanced by planting them near bold-textured plants or other objects that contribute strong, solid form to the garden, such as rocks, ponds or structures.

Grasses lack the broad-petalled, colorful flowers typical of other perennials, but their delicate, tiny flower parts have a special beauty. When they dry and become translucent, the flower parts glow in the sunlight like the best fiber optics money can buy. The foliage of many grasses is translucent, as well, and can offer similar magical effects. I always try to place grasses to take advantage of back- or sidelighting.

As the wind plays with their limber stalks and leaves, grasses bring a special dynamism to the garden. I take great pleasure in the way swaying grasses make my garden feel alive and responsive. This is especially important in the winter, when a patch of dancing grasses may tempt me outdoors for a walk.

Variations in form, scale, texture and foliage color are more important with plants such as grasses, whose primary strength is not flower color. Grasses range from fountain-like to mounding to nearly-bolt-upright in form, from diminutive to gigantic in scale, and from fine to coarse in texture. In addition to a myriad of greens, summer foliage colors include subtle shades of blue, white, yellow and red, often followed in autumn by rich shades of orange, burgundy and gold.

Designing with grasses

When you first consider the role grasses will play in your garden, keep in mind that most ornamental grasses are garden perennials, and many of the principles of gardening with perennials apply equally to grasses. The most common mistake is to segregate grasses from the rest of the garden. A bed made solely of perennial flowers is a high-maintenance bore, and a garden composed entirely of grasses is equally laborious and one-dimensional.

When I first began to study grasses in the native American landscape, I noticed that they occur most often in huge sweeps and masses. Such grand gestures seem appropriate to this big country and our national character. Space permitting, many ornamental grasses are best used this way in the garden, but some are equally effective planted as single specimens or in small groupings.

Observing the native landscape also has taught me how happily the grasses' peak periods of interest correspond with the glory of our Eastern autumn and the challenge of our winter. Most grasses make perfect companions for bright autumn foliage and vivid fall-bloomers. Later, grasses add their winter hues of chestnut, fawn and russet to the ivories, browns and reds of the usual bark and berry brigade.

Grasses add a graceful look to gardens in warmer-winter climates as well. There, a more gradual drop in fall

Grasses can be quite effective when they're planted alone. Here, a specimen of miscanthus 'Morning Light' is highlighted against its darker surroundings.

The flowers and seed heads of many grasses are intriguing and invite close inspection. Here, the setting sun majestically illuminates the seed heads of wild-oat.

With its feathery flowers, bright fall foliage and compact size, miscanthus 'Purpurascens' is an ideal grass for smaller gardens.

temperatures causes some grasses to develop better fall color. In milder-winter areas, certain grasses that are deciduous in our climate are evergreen or semi-evergreen.

Grasses can be used in informal or formal settings with equal success. Here in the formally-designed Longwood Gardens where I work as the Curator of Plants, grasses are superbly presented in deep borders that allow the larger ones to grow to full size and still be in scale. The grasses remain in place through the seasons amid successive plantings of flowering plants. Excellent descriptions of ornamental grasses at Longwood and their uses can be found in *Idea Garden Ornamental Grasses*, available for $4.00 including postage (PA residents, $4.12), from the Longwood Gardens Museum Shop, P.O. Box 501, Rt. 1, Kennett Square, PA 19348-0501.

Some favorite grasses

My partner, Claire Sawyers, and I have had two gardens

Dramatic seedstalks rise above two ornamental grasses, *Molinia* 'Skyracer' (left) and *Spodiopogon sibiricus* (back), in a border in the author's garden.

in the decade since I began growing ornamental grasses. The first one, in Newark, Delaware, encompassed less than one-eighth of an acre. The heavy clay soil was too great a challenge for many perennials, but the grasses generally proved adaptable. A few of them became clear favorites. Wild-oat (*Chasmanthium latifolium*), an upright, medium-textured grass, became a lovely focal point under dogwood trees lining a front walk. This durable native American grass tolerated the partial shade and root competition of the dogwoods while retaining good, green leaf color. In summer we enjoyed its attractive oat-like spikelets, and in fall the plants turned a warm gold, glowing in the setting sun just as we arrived home. Each spring it reliably produced more seedlings than we could give away, but not so many that it was a nuisance.

We also became enamored of Foerster's feather-reed grass (*Calamagrostis × acutiflora* 'Karl Foerster'). Widely, but incorrectly, sold as 'Stricta', this sterile hybrid rates near the top of all the grasses. By April it produces a neat mound of fine-textured, dark green foliage. The flowers are purplish and open as soon as they appear in June. By August, they dry and stiffen into tawny, upright wands which remain attractive throughout winter, as does the almost-evergreen basal foliage. Although it does best in full sun, 'Karl Foerster' performed well in as much as half shade—flowering was not as full, but the plants remained upright.

A third favorite was *Miscanthus* 'Purpurascens'. Among the most compact miscanthus available, it is ideal for smaller gardens. Flowering relatively early, usually in late

July or early August, the plant barely tops 5 ft. Upright and narrow in form, this cultivar thrived in full sun, but also grew well in one-third shade. With sufficient moisture, our plants in full sun turned bright orange-red each fall, more brilliant than any other miscanthus. Plants growing in shade turned pleasing hues of pastel pink, salmon, gold and cream. 'Purpurascens' is less drought-tolerant than most miscanthus—one year an overly-dry summer and early onset of cold weather resulted in scorched foliage and very little fall color.

Two years ago we moved to 1½ acres in Landenberg, Pennsylvania. The larger space has been a joy, providing room for experimenting with new grasses and suitable companion plants. This garden is much sunnier than our last one, and the soil is rich, well-drained loam.

Here is just one example of the many ways we've included grasses in our new garden. In a bed alongside the back of the house, the slender flower stalks of a specimen plant of tall moor grass (*Molinia caerulea* subsp. *arundinacea* 'Skyracer') shoot 8 ft. into the August sky, surrounded by river birches, Virginia sweetspire and fothergilla. Its fine texture and strong sculptural form play well against a nearby specimen of giant coneflower (*Rudbeckia maxima*), whose large, yellow flowers are borne on sturdy, tall stalks throughout July and August. The birch bed is in its full glory in October and November, when the clear golden-yellow of 'Skyracer' contrasts with the dark purple-bronze sweetspire and the red-orange fothergillas.

As I've come to know the grasses better, I've learned to appreciate the subtler ones. Autumn moor grass (*Sesleria autumnalis*) is an underused gem, with attractive upright seed stalks that last throughout the winter. Forming a neat, tufted mound of light-green to chartreuse foliage, it is a superb edging plant for half shade, though it will tolerate nearly full sun. Another wonderful grass, *Spodiopogon sibiricus*, fits well into the same cultural niche, growing into a neat, rounded plant about 3 ft. high. Its fuzzy, upright flower stalks appear in August, and the plant often takes on orange and red tones in September.

Although it's hard to love a plant that aggressively crushes or shades its neighbors, I've learned to appreciate the beauty of Korean feather-reed grass (*Calamagrostis arundinacea* var. *brachytricha*), which gently leans on nearby plants. It has an almost explosive form, sending light pink puffs of flowers out in all directions in September. It is delightful when, after a rain, it gracefully rests on the wine-colored tops of sedum 'Autumn Joy' or when its flowers poke through the winged branches of a nearby euonymus, whose delicate salmon fall leaf color brings out the pink of the grass.

Growing grasses

Many grasses can be successfully propagated by seed, but most gardeners will probably want to purchase plants in order to get named cultivars with special qualities. (See mail-order sources listed at right.)

Culturally, grasses are a forgiving group, and the basics of their care are easy to master. Grasses vary considerably in their drainage requirements—many of the larger ones, such as miscanthus, tolerate saturated soils, while smaller, tufted types, such as the fescues, will quickly succumb to an overabundance of moisture, especially during the winter. Select those that are suited to your conditions.

Grasses adapt well to different soil types—most appreciate a good loam but also will grow in heavy clays or even in sand. The majority of true grasses are native to

A sweep of Foerster's feather reed grass (background) and Scottish tufted hair grass 'Schottland' (foreground) looks as appealing in mid-May (top) as it does when the plants flower in August (below).

SOURCES

The following mail-order nurseries specialize in ornamental grasses, offering a wide or unusual selection.

Andre Viette Farm and Nursery, R.D. 1, P.O. Box 16, Fisherville, VA 22939, 703-943-2315. Catalog $2.00.

Kurt Bluemel, Inc., 2740 Greene Lane, Baldwin, MD 21013. Catalog $2.00.

Greenlee Nursery, 301 E. Franklin Ave., Pomona, CA 91766, 714-629-9045. Catalog, descriptive, $5.00.

Limerock Ornamental Grasses, Inc., R.D. 1, Box 111-C, Port Matilda, PA 16870, 814-692-2272. Catalog $2.00.

Niche Gardens, 1111 Dawson Road, Chapel Hill, NC 27516, 919-967-0078. Catalog $3.00.

Prairie Nursery, P.O. Box 306, Westfield, WI 53964, 608-296-3679. Catalog $3.00, 2 yr.

Prairie Ridge Nursery, R.R. 2, 9738 Overland Rd., Mt. Horeb, WI 53572, 608-437-5245. Catalog $1.00.

Stock Seed Farms, Rt. #1, Box 112, Murdock, NE 68407, 402-867-3771. Catalog free.

sunny places. If they're planted in too much shade, their growth is weakened and they tend to fall over. As a guide, the wider the foliage of a particular grass, the greater its shade tolerance.

The fibrous root systems of grasses are very efficient, and once established, most grasses are as drought-tolerant as they are claimed to be. In general, the narrower the foliage, the greater the drought tolerance. Here in Pennsylvania, fall planting eliminates the need for irrigating most grasses once they've been watered-in after planting, as long as they're planted early enough for the roots to take hold before the first hard freeze and as long as rainfall amounts are normal. In

Korean feather-reed grass leans gracefully on sedum 'Autumn Joy'.

warmer climates, summer irrigation may be required, even with fall planting.

In two gardens and ten years, I've yet to buy my first bag of fertilizer. Ornamental perennial grasses just don't require it, unless you're gardening in sand. Excess fertility causes soft growth and a greater need for mechanical supports, and may, in some cases, introduce diseases into otherwise disease-free plants. (The only disease I've ever encountered has been foliar rust in wet summers, which can be minimized by spacing the plants properly and allowing adequate air movement.)

Mulch helps conserve water and control weeds, but not all grasses tolerate mulch equally well. Clump-forming grasses that are native to dry environments, such as the fescues, can easily be killed when mulch sits snug against the crown or forms a catch-basin. To be on the safe side, mulch only to within a few inches of the crown.

Other maintenance consists of little more than a yearly cutting back and some occasional dividing. Grasses don't require cutting back, although most gardeners prefer to do so for aesthetic reasons or to reduce the litter of the dried leaves.

I enjoy looking at many of the seed heads in winter, so I leave most grasses standing until March, when new growth begins. (If new growth emerges earlier or later in your climate, adjust the pruning time accordingly. Be sure to cut grasses back before new growth is tall enough to

interfere or be damaged.) At that time, I cut back the grasses close to the top of the crown, usually 3 in. to 6 in. from the ground. I use a hand clippers, although an electric hedge shears or even a small chain saw works better for very large plantings. Burning is an effective alternative if your local codes permit it.

Most grasses will grow at least a few years before they must be divided, but any grass that tends to die out in the center and become floppy will eventually require division. Many miscanthus can go five years or more without division, while fescues planted as ground cover may require dividing every third year to maintain a neat appearance. Some grasses, like *Molinia* 'Skyracer', seem to get bigger and better each year. My guess is that 'Skyracer' won't need dividing for a decade.

It's best to divide or transplant grasses during their active vegetative growth. For cool-season growers, such as fescues and feather-reed grasses, the proper time for these activities is in fall or spring; for warm-season growers, such as miscanthus or Indian grass (*Sorghastrum nutans*), divide or move in spring. Transplanting warm-season growers in the fall risks winter injury, especially in colder climates.

To divide a grass plant, I dig it up with a good amount of roots attached. Using my hands, a sharp spade, or sometimes, an ax, I pull or chop the clump into pieces, each composed of at least one stem, or culm, and

Encased in ice, a specimen of miscanthus 'Gracillimus' contributes to the beauty of the early spring landscape.

a few roots. If my main purpose is to renew the plant, I cut it into just a few pieces, which will quickly grow into good-sized plants. If I want to increase my stock, I'll make many smaller divisions.

The palette of cultivated hardy perennial grasses is rapidly expanding. In addition to recent introductions from Europe and Asia, there is a new focus on our neglected American flora that promises a wealth of new garden grasses. All of them offer exciting opportunities for American gardeners to add new dimensions to their gardens.   □

Rick Darke is Curator of Plants at Longwood Gardens in Kennett Square, Pennsylvania

Draping over a path, the gold, green and tan foliage of ornamental grasses hints at the landscaping potential of this diverse plant group.

Daffodils

Landscaping with easy-to-grow bulbs

by Brent and Becky Heath

Bright-yellow trumpet daffodils are a beloved sign of spring to gardeners across the country, and planting the bulbs is one of the easiest and most rewarding investments a gardener can make. What other plant can you buy for a dollar or so, stick in the ground with a minimum of fuss, and enjoy each spring for decades to come?

We're daffodil enthusiasts who delight in the luminous colors and penetrating fragrances of these flowers. We grow and sell bulbs, hybridize daffodils to breed new varieties, and design landscapes and garden settings that use daffodils. At our own farm, and in designing plantings for botanical gardens, commercial landscapes and private homeowners, we've practiced several methods of combining daffodils with other plants in the landscape. We use them to add spring color to meadows, woodlands, perennial bor-

ders and ground-cover beds, and as special focal points in a garden.

Our farm is located in the Tidewater area of Virginia. The early colonists introduced daffodils to this part of the world by planting bulbs of the small-flowered, sweet-scented daffodils called jonquils or "jonniquills." My (Brent's) grandfather, who had worked in overseas agriculture for the U.S. government, visited the area in 1900, and observed a cottage industry based on picking the flowers from naturalized plantings and sending them to market in Baltimore, along with other spring produce. He saw a chance to expand the industry, and began importing bulbs of bigger and better hybrid daffodil varieties from England and Europe and selling them to local farmers. Thanks to his efforts and the abilities of local growers, this area became the daffodil capital of the world by the 1920s. Sold as a cut flower,

Thousands of daffodils grow in the pondside meadow at the Heaths' farm in Virginia (above). Bulbs planted as long as 40 years ago have thrived with little maintenance other than annual mowing and fall fertilization.

the daffodil was the "poor man's rose."

Times changed and the daffodil cut-flower industry declined after World War II. My father got more involved in selling the bulbs themselves, and at one time he grew about 10,000 different varieties. I grew up with daffodils, and liked the flowers and the business, so I've stayed with it.

Most gardeners are surprised to learn that there are so many kinds of daffodils. Collectors group them into 12 "divisions" based on characteristics of the flowers: the length and shape of the corona or cup, the number of flowers per stem, the presence of double flowers, and other variations. All the many forms of daffodils are species or hybrids in the genus *Narcissus*. Native to Europe and the Mediterranean area, daffodils can be grown in most parts of the United States, except Florida and other subtropical areas. As garden plants, they vary in earliness, length of bloom, vigor and stature. In our garden, the earliest daffodils start flowering in February, and the latest last until May. Depending on the weather and the variety, individual flowers may fade in a week, or hold their beauty for a month.

Photos, pp. 84-85: Brent Heath

Some miniature daffodils are only 4 in. to 5 in. tall and have tiny flowers. The largest hybrids reach 18 in. to 20 in. tall, with flowers up to 5 in. in diameter.

Although yellow and white are the most common flower colors, shades of pink, red, orange or green appear in some varieties. Generally speaking, yellow daffodils bloom earlier than do white ones. White or pink daffodils usually start out yellow, then gradually change color after they've been open for a few days. Like colors, fragance differs among different daffodil varieties—some are lightly sweet, others so intense that a single blossom will perfume a whole room—and often the fragrance changes as the flowers age.

We like to use a wide assortment of daffodils, not just the common forms. Sometimes we look at a particular site and try to find the best daffodils to use there; other times we start with a special daffodil and try to find the best way to grow and display it.

"Naturalizing" daffodils is planting them so that they grow and look like wildflowers. Many people first think of naturalizing daffodils in a lawn. Indeed, a lawnful of daffodils is a breathtaking sight in early spring, but they cause a problem later in the season. The daffodil leaves need to grow six to eight weeks to store enough food to produce blooms for the next season. Meanwhile, the lawn grass is growing tall and shaggy. One solution is to plant the daffodils around the edge of the lawn and let that area grow up along with the bulb foliage, while grooming the center of the lawn. Another is to combine bulbs with late-developing grasses that don't grow and need mowing until the weather has warmed up and the daffo-

dils are nearly mature. Either way, it's advisable to choose cultivars that bloom early, are less than 10 in. tall and finish growing before it's time to mow the grass. 'February Gold', only 12 in. tall with yellow flowers, and 'Bambi', 8 in. tall with a white perianth and yellow trumpet, both flower in February at our farm.

If you want a big expanse of daffodils without the problems of putting them in a lawn, try combining daffodils with annual and perennial flowers and grasses to make meadow gardens. Over the last 30 to 40 years, my family has planted hundreds of different kinds of daffodils in a meadow around the pond on our farm (photo, facing page). No one went to any trouble to improve the sandy soil or to prepare the site, and we didn't plan out the area in advance; instead, the meadow has evolved gradually as we keep adding more bulbs or other plants.

Our daffodil meadow is a sight to behold in the spring, especially with the reflection in the water. Later in the season, the same scene is filled with daylilies, an assortment of natural and planted wildflowers, perennial sunflowers, and ornamental grasses. A few pines and several small deciduous trees cast a light shade in the summer. All we do to maintain the meadow is run the lawn mower over it in the fall and then spread a light application of 5-10-20 fertilizer. This is a low-maintenance garden: no watering, spraying, staking, pruning, weeding or mulching. We've never even dug and divided the bulbs.

We've experimented with many different kinds of daffodils to see which do best

Daffodils were once a mainstay of the cut-flower industry. Above, Becky Heath displays the many colors and forms of the blossoms.

in naturalized plantings. The best yellow daffodil for naturalizing is 'Carlton'. It's a fine soft-yellow color with a large cup, and has a delicious vanilla fragrance. 'Ceylon' is a good naturalizer with a yellow perianth and a reddish-orange cup that darkens as it matures. It has the longest-lasting flowers of any daffodil we grow—four weeks or more in a good year. Most double daffodils don't naturalize well, but 'Flower Drift', an orange, yellow and white double, is an exception. 'Yellow Cheerfulness', a fragrant yellow multi-blossomed double, is another fine naturalizer.

To create a naturalized planting, we start by evaluating the site. Naturally fertile soil with neutral pH is ideal, but daffodils will grow well in average soil that is slightly acid or alkaline. What's most important is picking a spot with good drainage and at least a half day's sun. Daffodils do fine along the edge of a woods, or underneath deciduous trees that don't leaf out until weeks after the flowers have bloomed.

Then we like to lay out graceful free-form shapes and fill them in with bulbs planted at about 6-in. spacing, not in rigid rows. Some gardeners just toss the bulbs over their shoulders and plant them where they fall, but often the results look patchy and irregular. Whichever way you design the planting, be generous with the bulbs, and use enough to make a big splash of color. We helped design a naturalized planting for a five-acre meadow area at Longwood Gardens, Pennsylvania, that looked like a river of daffodils, with 10,000 bulbs each of ten different cultivars (see photo, p. 86). In a home garden, you might try planting 50 or 100 bulbs apiece of several varieties.

When we're planting hundreds of

In this Longwood Gardens planting they helped with, the Heaths created a natural effect where the daffodils look like wildflowers. They laid out graceful curved shapes and filled in the areas with bulbs planted 6 in. apart.

It's easiest to plant large numbers of bulbs if two people work together—one to dig the holes, and the other to insert the bulbs (left). Some planting tools work better than others (above). A heavy-duty bulb planter with an offset footstep (on the left) is good for punching one hole after another, since the soil keeps pushing up and out the top. If the foot bar straddles the planter (center left), the soil can't come out at the top and you have to empty the planter after every hole you dig. A lightweight metal planter (center right) is liable to bend if you dig in heavy or rocky soil. A thistle fork (right) works like a chisel to pry open a slot in the soil big enough for a bulb.

SOURCES

You can buy bulbs of the more common daffodils at local garden centers in the fall. Select healthy bulbs that feel heavy and solid, not lightweight or shriveled, with no visible wounds and no evidence of powdery black or white fungal spores.

The price of a daffodil bulb depends on what variety it is and how large it is. Daffodil bulbs are graded by circumference and the number of "noses" or growing points. A #1 triple-nose or mother bulb usually produces three blooms the first year. (Be warned that "top size" is not standard terminology in grading daffodils, and doesn't equate with #1.) A #2 double-nose or garden-center-size bulb usually produces two blooms. A #3 round or landscape-size bulb produces a single bloom, and a chip or offset may or may not make a bloom the first year. If you buy smaller bulbs, they won't make as many flowers the first year, but with good care they'll soon increase.

If you plan ahead and order daffodils by mail, you can choose from a wider selection of varieties. Place your order in the spring or summer for fall delivery. Before ordering the rarer species of Narcissus, please inquire if the bulbs were propagated and grown in nursery conditions, not collected from wild populations, which are nearing extinction due to indiscriminate over-harvesting.

Among the large mail-order nurseries, Burpee Seeds (300 Park Ave., Warminster, PA 18974; catalog free) and Wayside Gardens (P.O. Box 1, Hodges, SC 29695; catalog $1.00) offer a good assortment of daffodils. Two daffodil specialists are The Daffodil Mart (Rt. 3, Box 794, Gloucester, VA 23061; catalog $1.00, color booklet $3.00) and Grant Mitsch Novelty Daffodils (P.O. Box 218A, Hubbard, OR 97032; catalog $3.00).

For more information on daffodils, write to The American Daffodil Society (c/o Leslie Anderson, Rt. 3, 2302 Byhalia Rd., Hernando, MS 38632; annual membership $15.00).

Photos: top, Brent Heath; others, Staff

Daffodils planted in a bed of ground covers add welcome spring color to the landscape. These 'Dove Wings' grow up between the runners of English ivy.

Clumps of daffodils are the first flowers to bloom in this garden. Later in the season, hostas, lilies, daylilies and other perennials fill in the bed and hide the withering daffodil leaves.

bulbs at a time, we prefer to work as a team, with one person digging the holes and the other handling the bulbs. For inserting bulbs into an area where other plants are already growing, we use a tool called a thistle fork. It has a 3-in. by 8-in. blade on a 3-ft. T-shaped handle, and a foot bar to step on. It's easy to jab it into the soil and pry an opening big enough to drop a bulb into. Measuring from the soil surface to the bottom of the hole, we plant the bulbs at a depth equal to three times their height—a bit shallower in heavy clay soils, or somewhat deeper in sandy soils.

If we're planting bulbs in soft, loose soil, we use a long-handled bulb planter that punches out a big cone of soil. This kind of planter is hard to use in compacted, rocky or root-filled soil, but it works great in freshly tilled planting areas. Again, one person makes the holes and the other person drops in the bulbs. As we quickly punch one hole after another, the soil tumbles out the top of the planter. Then when we're done planting, we rake the bed smooth again. If you're planting just a few bulbs, you'll get by with a lightweight, trowel-sized bulb planter, but if you've got a lot of bulbs to plant, using heavy-duty, long-handled tools makes the job faster and easier.

Daffodil bulbs should be planted in the fall, as soon as possible after the soil has started to cool off—the temperature should be 60°F at a depth of 6 in., if you want to check it with a soil thermometer. We start planting in September and often continue on into December. It's important for the daffodils to grow roots before the ground freezes. After they've rooted, they are quite cold-hardy, but unrooted bulbs are damaged by frost. If for some reason

you don't get around to planting bulbs in the fall, store them in a cool, dry place with good ventilation and plant them as early as possible in the spring. The first season, they'll flower late, on shorter stems than usual, but they should perform normally in future years.

We spread fertilizer as a topdressing after first planting bulbs, and again each subsequent fall. One feeding per year is sufficient. (Bulbs don't need to be fertilized in the spring; in fact, an excess of nitrogen in the spring will stimulate soft growth and make the bulbs vulnerable to disease.) Traditional garden lore recommends bone meal, but it really isn't a complete fertilizer for bulbs. It supplies phosphorus, but it lacks the other nutrients that the bulbs also need. We use a 5-10-20 slow-release fertilizer with trace elements, and apply about ½ cup per 10 sq. ft. Rainwater dissolves the fertilizer and carries it down to the bulbs' roots. We use the same fertilizer, always applied in the fall, for naturalized plantings and for more formal plantings in beds of ground covers or perennials.

Other than planting and fertilizing, naturalized daffodils hardly need any care. You can deadhead, or pull off the faded blooms, for cosmetic reasons, but it isn't necessary. Likewise, you can cut off the leaves as soon as they begin to yellow and flop over, if they look too untidy for your tastes, or you can just let the foliage wither away naturally.

With ground covers or in borders, daffodils add welcome spring color. White-flowered varieties such as 'Stainless' or 'Glacier' look expecially nice against the rich foliage of the evergreen ground covers. Other attractive combinations are

white or yellow daffodils with the lavender blooms of vinca, or with the purple blooms of violets or grape hyacinths. If you're starting a new bed, it's easy to plant the daffodil bulbs the same year you set out the ground-cover plants. We use the bulb planter to plug bulbs down into the loose, soft soil of a new bed. In established plantings of English ivy or vinca, the thistle fork is more convenient for prying openings between the runners.

During the summer, ground covers or other plants with dense foliage shade the soil and protect the dormant bulbs from too much heat. Most daffodils appreciate this respite. However, two divisions of daffodils, the jonquillas and the tazettas, benefit from a summer baking in warm soil. Combine them with other heat-loving plants such as succulents, and be sure to plant them where you can enjoy their fragrance. The jonquillas 'Sweetness' and 'Trevithian' have several golden-yellow blooms per stem, and a lovely sweet fragrance. The tazetta 'Geranium' displays a shallow deep-orange cup against a glossy-white perianth, and also bears several flowers per stem. All of these are excellent for planting on sites where the soil is hot and dry in the summer.

In perennial flower beds and borders, daffodils are ideal companions to peonies, hostas, irises, daylilies or lilies. They come up and flower much earlier than do most of the perennials, so they extend the season of bloom. Then as the bulbs finish blooming, the perennials obscure the declining daffodil foliage. Daffodils and perennials grow well together. Since the bulbs generally are planted about 6 in. to 8 in. deep, their roots don't compete for water or nutrients with the shallower roots of the perennials. Also, the daffodils make their active growth in the late fall and early spring, when the perennials are dormant; the perennials grow in the late spring and summer, when the daffodils are dormant.

We like to plant groups of at least six to ten bulbs of one cultivar, set at 6-in. spacing so they'll make a good show right away, and to position these clumps among the perennials in the bed. Grouping bulbs this way makes a more attractive display than would spreading them out to make little dabs of color here and there. If you can afford only a few bulbs or want to start small, try planting them near a point of interest such as a tree, rock or path. This is also a good way to show off a special variety, such as the lovely pink-cupped 'Pink Pride', the exotic red-and-yellow double 'Tahiti', or 'Red Hill', with its striking red cup against a glistening white perianth.

It's possible to grow daffodils in containers such as tubs and window boxes, if the plants aren't exposed to hard freezes or to alternate freezing and thawing in the winter. In mild climates, this isn't as much of a problem, but in cold climates, it's best to move the container next to a building and put a tarp or other covering over it for insulation. The bigger the container, the better—larger sizes have more thermal mass. With today's lightweight fiberglass containers and soilless potting mixes, even a large planter can be portable. Remember to water regularly when the daffodils are blooming in the spring, and to fertilize them in the fall.

Division is the major task in maintaining daffodils. Over the years, a single bulb can multiply to produce a large clump of bulblets. In small-flowered daffodils, these smaller bulbs may each produce a flower stalk. As long as they're flowering well, there's no reason to divide the clumps unless you want to spread the bulbs out over a larger area. They can go for decades without dividing, which makes them ideal for naturalizing.

Large yellow trumpet daffodils, on the other hand, won't flower well if the clumps are so crowded that individual bulbs don't get enough water and fertilizer. They may have smaller and fewer flowers, or they may produce only leaves. For the best bloom, large-flowered varieties usually require digging and dividing every three to five years.

The best time to do this is about eight weeks after bloom, when the foliage is starting to turn yellow but before it has died down to the ground. Pull up on the leaves with one hand while prying under the clump with a spade or a fork, and lift out the whole mass of bulbs and roots. As you shake off the loose soil, the bulbs should separate naturally. Don't try to cut

Divide crowded clumps of daffodils in early summer, when the leaves are starting to turn yellow. Lift the entire clump and shake it gently, untangling the roots and leaves, until it separates into a pile of individual bulbs. (Photo: Staff)

or break them apart—just untangle the roots and leaves. It's best to discard any bulbs that you accidentally damage, as they're liable to rot. Replant the intact bulbs right away if possible. If you must store them, be sure to "cure" them in a warm, dry place with good air circulation—we hang them in mesh bags or spread them out on screens, out of the direct sun. Curing hardens the bulbs so they don't bruise or rot as easily. Keep them dry until you can plant them in the fall.

Daffodils are one of the most trouble-free plants you can put in the garden. The bulbs contain a poisonous alkaloid that causes a narcotic-like stupor, so mammals such as deer, rabbits or voles avoid daffodils. (Fortunately, this substance tastes so bad that there is little danger of children ingesting the bulbs or the leaves.) Few insects attack them, either. The larva or maggot of the narcissus bulb fly can tunnel into the bulbs and eat them, but it isn't a common pest.

Watch out for basal rot, caused by the fungus *Fusarium oxysporum*, especially during hot, rainy summers. Infected bulbs turn reddish-brown, starting at the base, and quickly decay until all that's left is a dry shell filled with rotten material. If you find dead bulbs like this, burn or discard them. The disease spores persist in the soil for years, so it's best not to replant daffodils in an area where previous plantings have disappeared. Prevent basal rot by planting daffodils in well-drained soil, not fertilizing them in the spring, and handling the bulbs carefully when you plant or divide them. With this minimal care, your bulbs should thrive. □

Brent and Becky Heath own and operate The Daffodil Mart in Gloucester, Virginia.

How daffodils grow

Daffodils begin an annual growth cycle when the bulbs put out new roots in the fall. This is the time to fertilize. The roots take up nutrients and water throughout the winter, except when the ground is frozen. During the winter, leaf and flower buds inside the bulb are getting ready to expand rapidly as soon as the soil warms up. The leaves penetrate above ground in early spring and quickly reach their full height, then the flower stalk shoots up and the flowers open. At this time, moisture is important; dry weather from March to May can reduce the number and size of the flowers.

After the flowers fade, the leaves continue to produce carbohydrates that are stored in the bulb. Sunlight and water are most important in this stage of the growth cycle. The foliage stays green for about eight weeks, then gradually turns yellowish brown and shrivels up. The roots also wither at this time.

Daffodils appear to be dormant during the next few months of midsummer and early fall, when, for commercial purposes, the bulbs are dug, shipped and sold. But deep inside, near the base of a bulb, is a growing point—a cluster of cells that are dividing and forming the buds for the next year's growth. Each growing point can produce three or four leaves and a single flower stalk with one or more flowers. If you were to slice open a bulb in the fall, you could determine the number of flower buds by counting the spots of bright-gold pollen, which shows up clearly against the plain white of the bulb's interior.

About the same time as the leaf and flower buds are forming, the bulb can also initiate an offset—a new growing point that later becomes a separate bulb. Given adequate water and nutrients, a bulb can form one new offset each year. At first, offsets are attached to the mother bulb at the base and enclosed within its brown sheathing scales. Each offset sends up just leaves for two or three years, then produces its first flower stalk. By then it will have grown into a bulb with its own basal plate and roots, separate from the mother bulb. New bulbs that form by division are identical to the parent bulbs.

Daffodils can also reproduce by seed. Species daffodils often are self-pollinating; the stigma picks up pollen as it emerges between the stamens. Such daffodils readily produce seeds and self-sow in a garden. Hybrid daffodils usually don't set seeds; they need cross-pollination, but infrequently are pollinated by insects. Daffodil breeders like ourselves produce new hybrids by hand-pollination, transferring the pollen from one flower to the stigma of another.

If the pollination is successful, the fruit capsule (seedpod) develops over the next six to eight weeks and opens in mid-May, before the foliage has died down. It contains as many as 50 seeds, small and round like fleshy peppercorns. We collect the seeds and sow them as soon as possible, and they usually begin to germinate after several months. We accelerate the seedlings' development by growing them in a warm, moist greenhouse for two or more years without any dormant periods. After we transplant them into nursery beds outside, they grow another two or three years before flowering.   —B.H. and B.H.

Illustration: Steve Buchanan

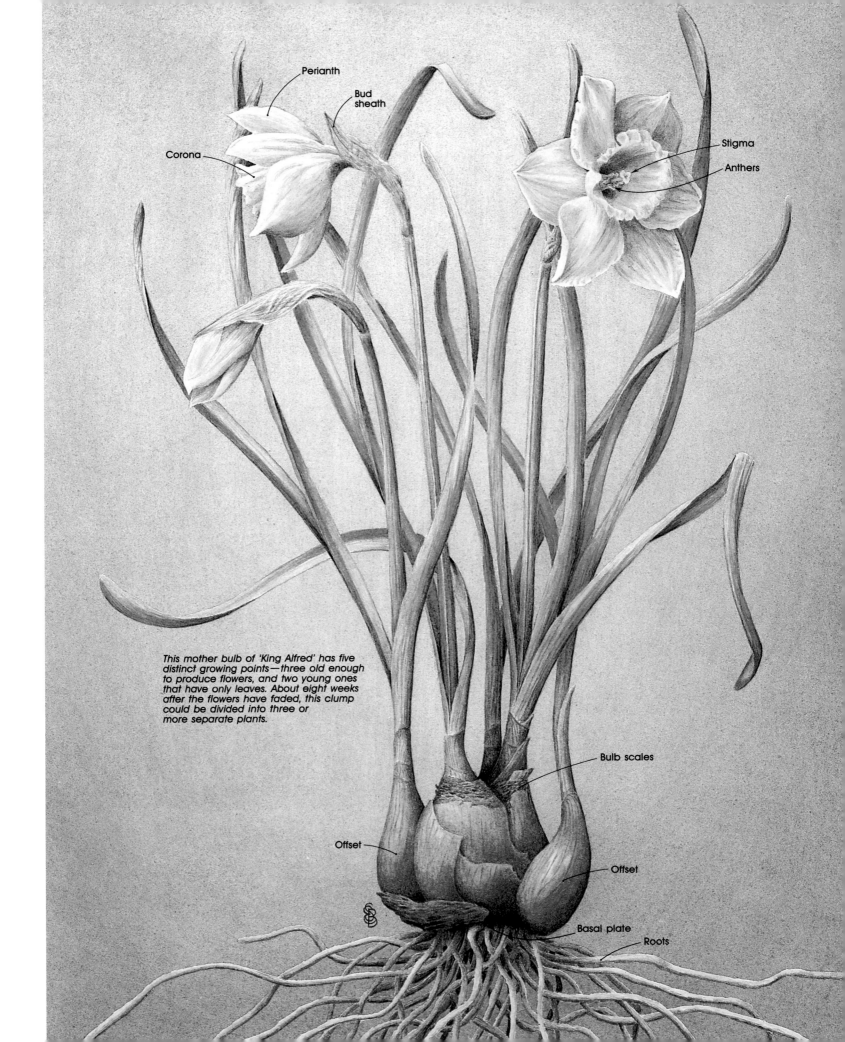

Perianth

Bud sheath

Corona

Stigma

Anthers

This mother bulb of 'King Alfred' has five distinct growing points—three old enough to produce flowers, and two young ones that have only leaves. About eight weeks after the flowers have faded, this clump could be divided into three or more separate plants.

Bulb scales

Offset

Offset

Basal plate

Roots

The Last and the First

Perennials for the other half of the year

by Edith R. Eddleman

Gardeners in the South and Pacific Northwest know that the gardening year has no beginning or end. My own garden is located in the Piedmont region of North Carolina, in the warmer part of the new USDA Zone 7. The soil seldom freezes here, but we often see temperatures of 0°F, and the all-time low is -9°F. Having seen winter temperatures plummet from 80°F to below freezing within hours, I like to refer to our climate as the temperamental zone. Fortunately, many plants can tolerate fluctuating temperatures and still flower or produce beautiful leaves in fall and winter.

Each of the plants described below offers something special—flowers, fruit or foliage—during that time when fall merges into winter and winter fades into spring. All adorn my garden during this season, which my friend the garden writer Ann Lovejoy calls "the other half of the year." I've listed the plants from earliest to latest. Some are difficult to find, but they are worth the search (see Sources on p. 93).

While it's rewarding to find a single flower in bloom on a gray, winter day, it is even more pleasing to experience plants in groupings where each plant gains by its association with others. Besides the plants I'll describe in detail, I'll mention other plants that combine well with them. There are an infinite number of combinations—experiment on your own. When you're browsing in catalogs, look for plants that flower exceptionally late in the fall, or early in the spring. Also consult one of the excellent books on the subject (see More Reading on p. 93).

Crimson flag. *Schizostylis coccinea* 'Oregon Sunset'. Zone 6.

This member of the iris family resembles a dainty gladiolus, with narrow leaves that form an 18-in.-tall clump. Buds appear on 2-ft.-tall stalks in October and November, and open to satiny-textured flowers of a delightful coppery red that combines equally well with hot colors and pastels.

For example, one of my plantings intermingles *S. coccinea* 'Oregon Sunset' and red-bladed Japanese blood-grass (*Imperata cylindrica* 'Red Baron'). It is fronted with clumps of *Euphorbia palustris*, whose chartreuse bracts created a sensational effect when this spurge bloomed out of season this past fall. Behind 'Oregon Sunset' and 'Red Baron', a clump of reblooming lavender-and-white bearded iris is flanked by silver-leafed artemisia 'Powis Castle' and chrysanthemum 'Mei Kyo'. Flowers of this chrysanthemum are raspberry colored when they open, but fade to pink and then to white with time.

In its native South Africa, *S. coccinea* grows in wet

Nestled among 18-in.-tall leaves, the iris-like, coppery-red blossoms of crimson flag 'Oregon Sunset' appear in October and November.

areas, often rooting in water. I've found that the plant adapts well to drier soils, but appreciates extra water, especially during the month preceding flowering and during flowering. It spreads by thin, white, rhizomatous roots, and multiplies fairly quickly. Although the species is hardy in Zone 6, it usually fails to flower there before frost. It is a reliable bloomer in Zone 7.

Arum italicum 'Pictum'. Zone 6.

My beginnings in horticulture were as a grower of tropical plants in greenhouse and apartment. *Arum italicum* 'Pictum' was the first hardy garden plant that intrigued me and drew me outdoors. Its arrowhead-shaped leaves, marbled with cream-colored veins, made it the most spectacularly beautiful plant I'd ever seen. It grew in my Great-aunt Edith's garden, in a raised bed covered in English ivy, beneath an ancient maple.

This arum produces icy-green, hooded spathes in May, followed by green fruits which ripen to orange-red by fall. The foliage vanishes in early summer but reappears with the first fall rains and persists until the next summer. On extremely cold mornings, my arum plants wilt to the ground, but as the day warms, the leaves gradually straighten up and return to normal.

A. italicum needs a moist, rich soil and loves compost. It does not enjoy my sandy, dry soil. My father grows spectacular plants in pots of pure compost. He also grows them outdoors in a nutrient-rich, heavy clay that is moist during the winter. Arum grows well in winter sun or in partial shade. In my garden I interplanted *A. italicum* 'Pictum' with the dainty, green-flowered *Helleborus viridis*, the chartreuse foliage of *Milium effusum* 'Aureum' and blue-flowered *Primula vulgaris* (the first primula to flower in my garden in spring). The inspiration for this combination came from "The Green Tapestry," a book by the English gardener Beth Chatto.

The arrow-shaped, marbled leaves of Italian arum pop up with the first fall rains and persist through the winter.

Climbing aster. *Aster carolinianus*. Zone 7.

This is an unusual aster, with woody, twining stems that branch repeatedly and can grow to 6 ft. or more. The plant covers itself with starry, lavender-pink flowers in the fall. Its leaves turn deep purple in autumn and drop in winter. Treat this plant like a shrub, thinning the stems only if need be. Do not cut the stems back at the end of the season as is done with other asters.

Aster carolinianus is a tough plant. Last year, after the brutally cold December of 1989, it opened new flowers on January 20. It is an uncommon native of marshes and low woodlands in the coastal Carolinas, but propagates easily and adapts to drier conditions.

In the Early/Late Border of the North Carolina State University Arboretum, *A. carolinianus* is trained through the branches of beautyberry (*Callicarpa americana*). In the autumn, the aster's flowers complement the red-violet color of the shrub's ripening berries. The two are underplanted with a carpet of *Ajuga* 'Burgundy Glow'.

Ligularia tussilaginea. Zone 7.

Ligularia tussilaginea produces low, 2-ft.-wide clumps of rounded, leathery, evergreen leaves the size of saucers. In October and November, buds on 2-ft.-tall stems open into single, butter-yellow flowers borne in loose clusters. The plant prefers moist but well-drained soil, and flowers well in open shade. Given a soil with an abundance of organic matter and moisture, the clumps can reach huge proportions.

There are several cultivars of *L. tussilaginea*. The variety 'Aureo-maculata', usually called the leopard plant, is

In November, clusters of small yellow flowers rise on 2-ft.-tall stems from a vigorous *Ligularia tussilaginea*. The low, leathery leaves are the size of saucers.

a familiar windowsill plant to some gardeners. Its green leaves have spots of pure gold. The leaves of 'Chirmen' are sparsely covered with soft, downy hairs, and they have ruffled, crested edges. The cultivar 'Argentea' has leaves of grey-green marbled with white. In a friend's garden, it combines well with a background of 'Glacier' English ivy, whose leaves are similar in color and pattern but of contrasting shape.

On 4-in. stems, the cream-white flowers of *Crocus ochroleucus* bloom in mid-November in the author's garden.

Crocus ochroleucus. Zone 6.

Elizabeth Lawrence, author of "A Southern Garden," described *Crocus ochroleucus* as a "pallid wraith." It has long, elegant buds which open to small, pearly-white flowers with throats the color of egg yolks. (The species name *ochroleucus* means yellow-white.) Plants flower in mid-November, but if cold weather slows them down, they may flower into the new year. At the base of a crape myrtle, I have interplanted them with *Crocus chrysanthus* 'Cream Beauty', whose pale, creamy-yellow flowers open in February.

Photos: left and top right, Edith Eddleman; below right, Pamela Harper

Iris unguicularis. Zone 7.

This is a lovely winter-flowering iris from Algeria, with narrow, flat leaves that grow to 2 ft. tall (the height depends on the cultivar). The flower buds first appear in October

A clump of *Iris unguicularis* blooms in profusion. This iris species flowers all winter in Zone 7 and is available in several cultivars.

and are produced throughout the winter, opening in mild spells through March. The flowers, typically a soft, violet color, nestle in the foliage. (Like crocuses, *I. unguicularis* bears flowers on flower tubes rather than on stems.) I pick buds, bringing them indoors where the flowers unfurl, releasing the scent of sweet violets in the warmth of the room.

There are many cultivars, which vary in flower color and in fragrance. In my garden, *I. unguicularis* `Walter Butt' is the earliest to flower. Its blossoms are white with a blush of lavender on some of the petals.

I. unguicularis is perhaps best grown in southern states and on the West Coast. (I am told that the plants have naturalized in San Francisco.) In the cold of Zone 6, the foliage survives, but the flower buds turn to mush. In Zone 7, the leaves are evergreen, but not ever beautiful: the tips often brown in our fluctuating winter cold.

The plant likes moderately-rich, well-drained soil, and a spot that is sunny in winter and a bit shady in summer. Plant it in a protected space near a door that you use frequently, so that you can enjoy the flowers all winter. Divide the plant in fall, when its roots are growing actively. The divisions may sulk for a year or two, though a friend often divides this plant without loss of bloom.

Blooming-size plants can be produced from seed in two years. (Seed exchanges of plant societies are a good source.)

Crocus goulimyi. Zone 5.

Crocus goulimyi is one of the treasures of the autumn garden. While many commonly-grown autumn crocuses flower before their leaves have emerged, *C. goulimyi* produces leaves and flowers at the same time. The rounded, lavender-blue petals are touched with pink and carried on 7-in.-tall flower tubes (which function as stems), above clumps of green-and-white-striped foliage. Flowering may begin as early as mid-September and continues through October. Each corm produces several flowers.

The purple flowers of *Crocus goulimyi*, which blooms in late fall, push through a carpet of creeping phlox.

C. goulimyi is easily grown and multiplies rapidly. It flowers well in full sun or in the light shade of deciduous trees and shrubs. Plant this crocus with oakleaf hydrangea (*Hydrangea quercifolia*). The crocus looks beautiful against this shrub's rosy-red, maroon and purple autumn foliage. Or interplant it with groundcovers that feature distinctive leaf colors: *Ajuga* `Burgundy Glow' with its pink, green, and cream leaves; or the ivy *Hedera helix* `Lemon Swirl', which continues to produce pale-lemony, new leaves through the fall. Or plant *C. goulimyi* among the corms of ivy-leaved *Cyclamen hederifolium*, whose dainty, pink flowers appear with those of the crocus. As an added bonus, the marvelously marbled green-and-silver leaves produced after the cyclamen flowers will persist throughout the winter.

A stand of sweet box carpets the ground. Its tiny, hidden flowers are intensely fragrant and scent the whole garden from late winter to spring.

Sweet box. Sarcococca hookerana var. humilis. Zone 6.

This delightful shrub is a member of the box family. It grows 18 in. to 2 ft. tall, and has wonderfully fragrant white flowers, which inspire its common name, sweet box. Buds form in November, and flowers open from late winter into spring, scenting the garden. The flowers are carried beneath the leaves, making the source of the fragrance a mystery. I have planted sweet box at the entrance to my garden so that passersby would be able to enjoy its fragrance.

Sweet box has distinctive, shiny, green foliage. It spreads by rhizomatous roots. It likes a loose, humusy soil, and particularly appreciates moisture in the spring when it's growing actively. It should be protected from the winter sun. I have read that it is hardy to Zone 5, but I think it would survive there only with winter snow cover. A friend in Zone 6 grows sweet box in a shaded area, but even there it dies to the ground in a severe winter.

Photos: top, J. C. Raulston; below, Pamela Harper

Helleborus foetidus. Zone 5.

Every year, *Helleborus foetidus* sends up clumps of new stems up to 2 ft. tall, with beautiful, palmate, shiny, green leaves. Buds enclosed in pale green bracts appear in November, and open in winter to form dangling clusters of green bells lipped in red. Given rich, humusy soil, a single clump may produce as many as five or six flowering stems, but two or three are more common. Hellebore flowers persist a long time, often into spring. After the plant sets seeds, its stems die to the ground. Simultaneously, new leaves emerge, so the plant is never without foliage.

My hellebores grow under a ligustrum that is trained as a 15-ft.-tall evergreen tree. Beneath and around the hellebores can be seen the lacy foliage and white flowers of *Isopyrum biternatum*, a small, native shrub. Clumps of the Lent lily (*Narcissus pseudonarcissus*), planted nearby, flower along with the hellebores in January and February.

Lesser celandine. *Ranunculus ficaria*. Zone 5.

Heart-shaped, green leaves marbled in silver emerge from the tuberous roots of lesser celandine in fall. The species has flowers that are a glistening, bright yellow. My plants begin to bloom in February, and go dormant by the end of May. Lesser celandine has a reputation as a first-rate garden bully, and I have seen sites where it has spread vigorously, but it has shown no thuggish tendencies in my own garden to date.

Many cultivars of *R. ficaria* are available from English nurseries, but an import permit is necessary to order them from these sources. Frequently, these cultivars can be found at the rare plant sales of botanical gardens and plant societies. The cultivar 'Flore-pleno' has bright yellow, double blooms. 'Major' bears large, yellow flowers on 10-in. stems. 'Aurantiaca' has lovely pale-orange flowers and silvery green leaves. 'Brazen Hussy', named by English gardener and author Christopher Lloyd, has deep bronze foliage and brilliant, lacquer-yellow flowers. 'Albus', 'Primrose' and 'Lemon Queen' offer flowers varying from cream to soft yellow. These combine along my garden path with *Primula* × *tommasinii*, blue *Phlox divaricata*, bronze-leaved *Ajuga*, and *Viola odorata* 'Royal Robe'.

Growing fall and winter plants helps me enjoy the season of short days and long nights. As I write at the end of a long, golden fall, I am waiting for the first flowers of the hybrid hoop-skirt daffodil, *Narcissus bulbocodium* 'Nylon', to shake out their lemony-yellow petticoats. They usually begin to bloom around December 8, but every winter can bring surprises. Part of the adventure of gardening is in not knowing what the season will bring; but part of the satisfaction of gardening is knowing that every season will bring delight. ☐

Edith R. Eddleman is a garden designer in Durham, North Carolina, and co-curator with Doug Ruhren of the renowned perennial borders at the NCSU Arboretum in Raleigh.

SOURCES

The numbers after each perennial refer to the sources below.

Arum italicum 'Pictum', 1.

Aster carolinianus, 5.

Crocus goulimyi, 4, 6, 7.

Crocus ochroleucus, 6, 4, 7.

Helleborus foetidus, 1.

Iris unguicularis, 5.

Ligularia tussilaginea, 3, 8.

Ranunculus ficaria, 8.

Sarcococca hookerana humilis, 1, 8.

Schizostylis coccinea 'Oregon Sunset', 2.

1. Forestfarm, 990 Tetherow Road, Williams, OR 97544. Catalog $3.00.

2. Gossler Farm and Nursery, 1200 Weaver Rd., Springfield, OR 97478-9663. Catalog $1.00.

3. Louisiana Nursery, Rt. 7, Box 43, Opelousas, LA 70570. Catalog $5.00, refundable.

4. McClure & Zimmerman, 108 W. Winnebago, P.O. Box 368, Friesland, WI 53935. Catalog free.

5. Montrose Nursery, P.O. Box 957, Hillsborough, NC 27278. Ask for Fall catalog, $2.00.

6. John Scheepers, Inc., P.O. Box 700, Bantam, CT 06750. Write for price.

7. The Daffodil Mart, Route 3, Box 794, Gloucester, VA, 23061. Ask for the botanical list, free.

8. Woodlanders, Inc., 1128 Colleton Ave., Aiken, SC 29801. Catalog in September, $1.00.

MORE READING

Here are several books about plants for the fall and winter garden. The first two books are in print. For the others, check libraries and used book sellers.

The Garden in Autumn, by Allan Lacy. The Atlantic Monthly Press, 19 Union Square West, New York, NY 10003; $29.95 hardbound.

Gardens in Winter, Elizabeth Lawrence. Claitor's Publishing Division, P.O. Box 3333, Baton Rouge, LA 70821. $12.50 ppd., hardbound.

Colour in the Winter Garden, by Graham Stuart Thomas. J. M. Dent & Sons Ltd., London, England. 3rd. ed., 1984. Out of print.

Flowers in the Winter Garden, by M.M. Graft. Doubleday & Co., Garden City, NY. 1966. Out of print.

Winter Blossoms from the Outdoor Garden, by A. W. Darnell. L. Reeve & Co. Ltd., Ashford, Kent, England. 1926. Out of print.

The Year-Round Bulb Garden, by Brian Mathew. Souvenir Press, London, England, 1986. Out of print.

The marbled leaves of the lesser celandine emerge from tuberous roots in late winter or early spring, followed quickly by daisy-like flowers.

Photo: Pamela Harper

Index

A

American Daffodil Society, address for, 86
American Hemerocallis Society, address for, 45
American Hosta Society, address for, 60
American Penstemon Society, address for, 67
American Peony Society, address for, 30
American Primrose Society, address for, 75
American Rock Garden Society, address for, 75
Armitage, Allan, M., on yarrows, 68-71
Arum italicum 'Pictum', discussed, 91
Asters (*Aster* spp.):
  climbing (*A. carolinianus*), 91
  fungal diseases of, 22
  in the garden, 22
  growing, 22
  perennial species, 18-22
  sources for, 22
Astilbes (*Astilbe* spp.):
  dividing, 39
  in the garden, 37
  growing, 37-39
  sources for, 38
Autumn moor grass (*Sesleria autumnalis*), discussed, 81

B

Basal rot, control of, 13, 88
Beaubaire, Nancy, on growing herbaceous peonies in warm climates, 28
Botrytis leaf spot, control of, 13
Bulbs:
  planters for, 86-87
  for shade gardens, 52

C

Crimson flag (*Schizostylis coccinea* 'Oregon Sunset'), discussed, 90
Crocus:
  Crocus goulimyi, 92
  Crocus ochroleucus, 91
Cut flowers:
  peonies, 27
  yarrow, 68-71
Cyclamen (*Cyclamen* spp.):
  in the garden, 24-25
  hardy, 23-25
  list of hardy and semi-hardy species, 24
  society for, 25
  sources for, 25
  starting from seed, 25
Cyclamen Society, address for, 25

D

Daffodils:
  basal rot of, controlling, 88
  bulb grades of, 86
  dividing, 88
  landscaping with, 84-88
  naturalizing, 85-87
  society for, 86
  sources for, 86
Darke, Rick, on landscaping with ornamental grasses, 78-83
Daylilies (American Hemerocallis Society), source for, 45
Daylilies (*Hemerocallis* spp.):
  book on, 45
  cultural requirements of, 45
  described, 40
  in the garden, 41-45
  propagating, 45
  society for, 45
  sources for, 45
Design, with hostas, 56-58

E

Eddison, Sydney:
  on daylilies, 40-45
  on primroses, 72-77
Eddleman, Edith R., on perennials for late fall and early spring, 90-93
Everlastings, yarrow, 68-71

F

Feather-reed grass (*Calamagrostis* spp.), discussed, 80, 81

G

Gardening, in shade, 51-55
Grasses, ornamental:
  designing with, 79-81
  dividing, 82
  growing, cultivating, 81-82
  list of favorite ornamental grasses, 80-81
  sources for, 81
  special qualities of, 79
Ground covers, for shade gardens, 54

H

Harrap, David, on herbaceous peonies, 26-31
Haynes, Ariel, on violets, 14-17
Heath, Brent and Becky, on daffodils, 84-89
Hellebores (*Helleborus* spp.):
  Christmas rose (*H. niger*), 33
  Corsican (*H. lividus corsicus*), 33-34
  cultural requirements of, 35
  described, 32-33
  in the garden, 34-35
  H. foetidus, 93
  Lenten rose (*H. orientalis*), 33, 53
  sources for, 35
Hemerocallis. See Daylilies.
Hosta Book, The (Aden), source for, 60
Hostas:
  book on, 60
  dividing, 60
  in the garden, 56-58
  growing, 58-60
  pests and diseases of, 60
  society for, 60
  sources for, 60

I

International Violet Association, address for, 17
Iris unguicularis, discussed, 92

J

Jones, Sam and Carleen, on hostas, 56-61

K

Kelaidis, Gwen, on penstemons for the garden, 62-67
Kelaidis, Panayoti, on veronicas, 46-50

L

Lesser celandine (*Ranunculus ficaria*), discussed, 93
Ligularia tussilaginea, discussed, 91
Lilies (*Lilium* spp.):
  dividing, 12
  growing, 10-13
  hybrids of, 9
  pests and diseases of, 13
  recommended varieties, 12
  society for, 13
  sources for, 13
  See also Daylilies.

The 17 articles in this book originally appeared in *Fine Gardening* magazine.
The date of first publication, issue number and page numbers for each article are given below.

If you enjoyed this book, you're going to love our magazine.

A year's subscription to *Fine Gardening* brings you the kind of hands-on information you found in this book, and much more. In issue after issue—six times a year—you'll find articles on nurturing specific plants, landscape design, fundamentals and building structures. Expert gardeners will share their knowledge and techniques with you. They will show you how to apply their knowledge in your own backyard. Filled with detailed illustrations and full-color photographs, *Fine Gardening* will inspire you to create and realize your dream garden!

To subscribe, just fill out one of the attached subscription cards or call us at 1-203-426-8171. And as always, your satisfaction is guaranteed, or we'll give you your money back.

Taunton
BOOKS & VIDEOS
for fellow enthusiasts

The Taunton Press 63 S. Main Street, P.O. Box 5506, Newtown, CT 06470-5506

FINE GARDENING

Use this card to subscribe to *Fine Gardening* or to request information about other Taunton Press magazines, books and videos.

☐ 1 year (6 issues) $26
$32 outside the U.S.

☐ 2 years (12 issues) $42
$52 outside the U.S.

(U.S. funds, please. Canadian residents: GST included)

Name _____

Address _____

City _____

State _____ Zip _____

☐ My payment is enclosed. ☐ Please bill me.
☐ Please send me information about other Taunton Press magazines, books and videos.

I'm interested in:
1 ☐ sewing
2 ☐ home building
3 ☐ woodworking
4 ☐ gardening
5 ☐ other

BFG1

FINE GARDENING

Use this card to subscribe to *Fine Gardening* or to request information about other Taunton Press magazines, books and videos.

☐ 1 year (6 issues) $26
$32 outside the U.S.

☐ 2 years (12 issues) $42
$52 outside the U.S.

(U.S. funds, please. Canadian residents: GST included)

Name _____

Address _____

City _____

State _____ Zip _____

☐ My payment is enclosed. ☐ Please bill me.
☐ Please send me information about other Taunton Press magazines, books and videos.

I'm interested in:
1 ☐ sewing
2 ☐ home building
3 ☐ woodworking
4 ☐ gardening
5 ☐ other

BFG1

Taunton
M A G A Z I N E S
for fellow enthusiasts

NO POSTAGE
NECESSARY
IF MAILED
IN THE
UNITED STATES

BUSINESS REPLY MAIL
FIRST CLASS MAIL   PERMIT NO.19   NEWTOWN CT

POSTAGE WILL BE PAID BY ADDRESSEE

THE TAUNTON PRESS
63 SOUTH MAIN STREET
PO BOX 5506
NEWTOWN CT 06470-9955